麦格希 中英双语阅读文库

麦琪的礼物

美国名人短篇小说精选

第1辑

【美】德雷伯 (C. G. Draper) ●主编

李晓东●译

麦格希中英双语阅读文库编委会●编

全国百佳图书出版单位
吉林出版集团股份有限公司

图书在版编目（CIP）数据

美国名人短篇小说精选. 第1辑, 麦琪的礼物 / (美)德雷伯 (C. G. Draper) 主编 ; 麦格希中英双语阅读文库编委会编 ; 李晓东译. -- 2版. -- 长春 : 吉林出版集团股份有限公司, 2018.3（2022.1重印）
（麦格希中英双语阅读文库）
ISBN 978-7-5581-4743-2

Ⅰ. ①美… Ⅱ. ①德… ②麦… ③李… Ⅲ. ①英语—汉语—对照读物②短篇小说—小说集—美国 Ⅳ. ①H319.4：I

中国版本图书馆CIP数据核字(2018)第046018号

美国名人短篇小说精选　第1辑　麦琪的礼物

编：麦格希中英双语阅读文库编委会
插　　画：齐　航　李延霞
责任编辑：欧阳鹏
封面设计：冯冯翼
开　　本：660mm×960mm　1/16
字　　数：237千字
印　　张：10.5
版　　次：2018年3月第2版
印　　次：2022年1月第2次印刷

出　　版：吉林出版集团股份有限公司
发　　行：吉林出版集团外语教育有限公司
地　　址：长春市福祉大路5788号龙腾国际大厦B座7层
邮编：130011
电　　话：总编办：0431-81629929
发行部：0431-81629927　0431-81629921(Fax)
印　　刷：北京一鑫印务有限责任公司

ISBN 978-7-5581-4743-2　　定价：38.00元
　　举报电话：0431-81629929

前言 PREFACE

英国思想家培根说过：阅读使人深刻。阅读的真正目的是获取信息，开拓视野和陶冶情操。从语言学习的角度来说，学习语言若没有大量阅读就如隔靴搔痒，因为阅读中的语言是最丰富、最灵活、最具表现力、最符合生活情景的，同时读物中的情节、故事引人入胜，进而能充分调动读者的阅读兴趣，培养读者的文学修养，至此，语言的学习水到渠成。

“麦格希中英双语阅读文库”在世界范围内选材，涉及科普、社会文化、文学名著、传奇故事、成长励志等多个系列，充分满足英语学习者课外阅读之所需，在阅读中学习英语、提高能力。

◎难度适中

本套图书充分照顾读者的英语学习阶段和水平，从读者的阅读兴趣出发，以难易适中的英语语言为立足点，选材精心、编排合理。

◎精品荟萃

本套图书注重经典阅读与实用阅读并举。既包含国内外脍炙人口、耳熟能详的美文，又包含科普、人文、故事、励志类等多学科的精彩文章。

◎功能实用

本套图书充分体现了双语阅读的功能和优势，充分考虑到读者课外阅读的方便，超出核心词表的词汇均出现在使其意义明显的语境之中，并标注释义。

鉴于编者水平有限，凡不周之处，谬误之处，皆欢迎批评教正。

我们真心地希望本套图书承载的文化知识和英语阅读的策略对提高读者的英语著作欣赏水平和英语运用能力有所裨益。

丛书编委会

Contents

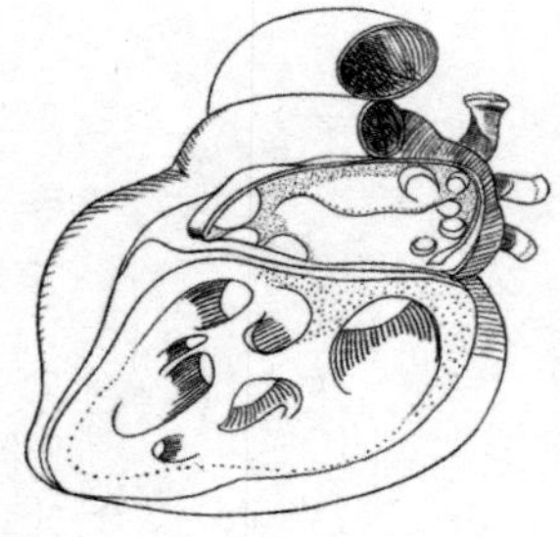

The Gift of the Magi

Adapted from the story by O.Henry

O. Henry's real name was William Sydney Porter. He was born in Greensboro, North Carolina, in 1862. He left school at the age of fifteen and worked in many different places. He also spent three years in ***prison*** because he took money from a bank. He started to write stories while he was in prison. O. Henry ***is famous for*** his stories with surprise endings. "The Gift of the Magi" is his most famous story. It is from the book *The Four Million*, stories about the everyday people of New York City. O. Henry died in 1910.

麦琪的礼物

根据欧·亨利同名故事改写

欧·亨利的真名是威廉·西德尼·波特，1862年生于北卡罗来纳州的格林斯波罗。他十五岁弃学，曾在很多地方工作，也曾因挪用公款而服刑三年。他在狱中开始写作。欧·亨利因其写的故事有意外的结局而闻名。《麦琪的礼物》是他最有名的作品《四百万》中的一篇，该书描述了纽约市日常生活中形形色色的人物。他逝世于1910年。

---

prison *n.* 监狱

be famous for 因……而著名

Della counted her money three times. She had only one dollar and eighty-seven cents. That was all. And tomorrow would be Christmas. What Christmas gift could she buy with only one dollar and eighty-seven cents? Della lay down on the old bed and cried and cried.

Let's leave Della alone for a while and look at her home. The chairs and tables were old and poor. Outside there was a ***mailbox*** without mail, and a door without a ***doorbell***. The name on the door said MR. JAMES DILLINGHAM YOUNG—Della's dear husband, Jim.

Della knew that Jim would be home soon. She dried her eyes and stood up. She looked in the ***mirror***. She began to ***comb*** her hair

---

黛拉把钱数了三遍，只有一元八角七，一分不多。明天就是圣诞节了，就这么一点钱能买什么礼物呢？她倒在那张破旧的长沙发上，不停地哭。

暂且不说黛拉，咱们来看看她的家吧：屋里的桌椅都很破旧；屋外有个信箱，可惜里面没有邮件；还有一扇门，但是没有门铃。门上写着：詹姆斯·迪灵汉·扬。这是指黛拉亲爱的丈夫——吉姆。

黛拉知道吉姆很快就要回来了。她赶紧擦干眼泪，站起身来，照照镜子，开始梳头，准备迎接吉姆。她心里很难过，因为她想为吉姆买一件像

---

mailbox *n.* 邮箱　　doorbell *n.* 门铃
mirror *n.* 镜子　　comb *v.* 梳头发

for Jim. She felt very sad. She wanted to buy Jim a Christmas gift—something good. But what could she do with one dollar and eighty-seven cents? She combed her hair in front of the mirror and thought. Suddenly she had an idea.

Now, Jim and Della had only two ***treasures***. One was Jim's gold watch. The other was Della's hair. It was long and brown, and fell down her back. Della looked in the mirror a little longer. Her eyes were sad, but then she smiled. She put on her old brown coat and her hat. She ran out of the house and down the street. She stopped ***in front of*** a door which said, MME. SOPHRONIE. HAIR OF ALL KINDS. ***Madame*** Sophronie was fat and seemed too white. The store was dark.

"Will you buy my hair?" Della asked.

样的圣诞礼物。可是，一元八角七又能买什么呢？她在镜子前一边梳头，一边琢磨。突然，她灵机一动，想出个主意来。

眼下，吉姆和黛拉只有两件值钱的东西，一是吉姆的金表，另一件是黛拉的头发。黛拉的头发是棕色的，长长的，一直垂到后背。她又在镜子前发了一会儿呆。她眼神虽然哀伤，但这会儿，却笑了。她穿上那件棕色的旧外衣，戴上帽子，从家里跑出去，来到大街上。她在一家小店门口停了下来，小店的门上写着：索芙尼太太，专收各种毛发。索芙尼太太很胖，皮肤显得过白。店里很阴暗。

"你想买我的头发吗？"黛拉问。

---

treasure *n.* 财产；珍品
madame *n.* （法语）夫人；太太
in front of 在……前面

"I buy hair," said Madame. "Take off your hat. Let's see your hair."

Della took off her hat. Her hair fell down like water. Mme. Sophronie lifted Della's hair with a heavy hand. "Twenty ***dollars***," she said.

"Give me the money now!" said Della.

Ah! The next two hours flew past like summer wind. Della shopped in many stores for the right gift for Jim. Then she found it—a ***chain*** for his gold watch. It was a good chain, strong and expensive. Della knew the chain would make Jim happy. Jim had a cheap chain for his watch, but this chain was much better. It would look good with the gold watch. The chain cost twenty-one dollars. Della paid for the chain and ran home with eighty-seven cents.

At seven o'clock Della made coffee and started to cook dinner.

"这儿是收头发，" 索芙尼太太说。"把帽子摘掉，我们看看货。"

黛拉摘掉帽子，她那长发像瀑布一样垂落下来。索芙尼太太用一只有力的大手掂了掂黛拉的头发后说："20美元。"

"我要现钱！"黛拉说。

哈！接下来的两个小时过得真像夏天里的风一样飞快。为了给吉姆买到合适的礼物，黛拉跑了很多商店。后来，她终于找到了——是一条与他的金表相匹配的表链。这条表链质地很好，做工结实，但价格非常昂贵。黛拉知道吉姆一见到它准会高兴。吉姆现在用的表链很便宜，但这条可就好多了，配他的金表正合适。这条表链的售价是21美元。黛拉交完钱，带着剩下的87美分跑回家了。

晚上七点，黛拉煮好咖啡，开始做晚饭。吉姆很快就要回来了，他从

---

dollar *n.* 美元　　**chain** *n.* 链条

Jim would be home soon. He was never late. Della heard Jim outside. She looked in the mirror again. "Oh! I hope Jim doesn't kill me!" Della smiled, but her eyes were wet. "But what could I do with only one dollar and eighty-seven cents?"

The door opened, and Jim came in and ***shut*** it. His face was ***thin*** and quiet. His coat was old, and he had no hat. He was only twenty-two. Jim stood still and looked at Della. He didn't speak. His eyes were strange. Della suddenly felt afraid. She did not understand him. She began to talk very fast. "Oh, Jim, dear, why do you look so strange? Don't look at me like that. I cut my hair and sold it. I wanted to buy you a Christmas gift. It will grow again—don't be angry. My hair grows very fast. Say 'Merry Christmas', dear, and let's be happy. You don't know what I've got for you—it's beautiful."

不晚归。黛拉听到了门外吉姆的声音，又照了照镜子。“哦！但愿吉姆别掐死我！”黛拉笑了，但眼睛却湿润了：“可是，仅有一元八角七，不这么办又能怎么样呢？”

门开了，吉姆走了进来，随手又把门关上。他的脸很瘦削，但很安详。他身上的外衣已经很旧了，头上没有戴帽子。他才22岁。吉姆站住了，静静地看着黛拉，一句话也不说，眼神很奇怪。黛拉有些紧张，她不明白吉姆为什么会这样。她开始急促地说：“哦，吉姆，亲爱的，你看上去怎么这么怪？别这样看我。我把头发剪下来卖掉了。我要给你买圣诞礼物。头发还会长出来的，别生气。我的头发长得很快。快说‘圣诞快乐’呀，亲爱的，咱们高兴点儿。你不知道我给你买了什么吧，可漂亮了！”

---

shut *v.* 关上　　　**thin** *adj.* 瘦的

"You cut your hair?" Jim spoke slowly.

"I cut it and sold it," Della answered. "Don't you like me now? I'm still me, aren't I?"

"You say that your hair is gone?" Jim asked again.

"Don't look for it, it's gone," Della said. "Be good to me, because it's Christmas. Shall we have dinner now, Jim?"

Jim seemed to wake up. He smiled. He took Della in his arms.

Let's leave them together for a while. They are happy, rich or poor. Do you know about the Magi? The Magi were wise men who brought Christmas gifts to the baby ***Jesus***. But they could not give gifts like Jim's and Della's. ***Perhaps*** you don't understand me now. But you will understand soon.

"你把头发剪了？"吉姆慢吞吞地说话了。

"我把它剪下来卖掉了，"黛拉回答说。"你不喜欢我了吗？我还是我，不是吗？"

"你是说你的头发没了？"吉姆又问了一遍。

"别找了，没了，"黛拉说。"今天是圣诞节，对我好点嘛。我们现在吃晚饭好吗，吉姆？"

吉姆好像突然间醒悟过来。他笑了，一把将黛拉抱在怀里。

我们就让这对夫妻甜蜜一会儿吧。他们是幸福的，且不说贫富。你听说过《圣经》中的麦琪，也就是东方三贤士吗？他们是为初生的耶稣送去圣诞礼物的智者。但他们却拿不出吉姆和黛拉那样的礼物。也许你现在还不能理解我的话，但过一会儿你就会明白的。

Jesus *n.* 耶稣

perhaps *adv.* 也许；可能

Jim took a small box out of his ***pocket***. "I love your short hair, Della," he said. "I'm sorry I seemed strange. But if you open the box, you will understand." Della opened the box. First she smiled, then suddenly she began to cry. In the box were two beautiful combs. Combs like those were made to hold up long hair. Della could see that the combs came from an expensive ***store***. She never thought she would ever have anything as beautiful! "Oh, Jim, they are lovely! And my hair grows fast, you know. But wait! You must see your gift." Della gave Jim the chain. The chain was bright, like her eyes. "Isn't it a good one, Jim? I looked for it everywhere. You'll have to look at the time one hundred times daily, now. Give me your watch. I want to see them together."

吉姆从衣袋里掏出一个小盒子。“我喜欢你的短发，黛拉，”他说。“对不起，我刚才的确有些怪。可是，你要是打开盒子的话，就什么都明白了。”黛拉打开盒子。她先是笑了，继而又哭了起来。盒子里有两把漂亮的梳子。那是用来拢住长发的梳子。黛拉看得出这种梳子是从高档商店里买来的。她从未幻想过她会有这么漂亮的东西！“哦，吉姆，它们真可爱！我的头发长得快，你知道。哦，等一下！你一定要看看我给你买的礼物。”黛拉把表链拿给吉姆。表链亮晶晶的，像黛拉的眼睛。“不好吗，吉姆？我跑了那么多地方，总算买到了。以后，你每天得看上百次才行。把表给我，我要把它们配在一起。”

---

pocket *n.* 口袋

store *n.* 商店

Jim *lay back* on the bed. He put his hands under his head, and smiled. "Della," he said, "let's put the gifts away. They are too good for us right now. I sold the watch to buy your combs. Come on, let's have dinner."

The Magi, as we said, were *wise* men—very wise men. They brought gifts to the baby Jesus. The Magi were wise, so their gifts were wise gifts. Perhaps Jim and Della do not seem wise. They lost the two great treasures of their house. But I want to tell you that they were wise. People like Jim and Della are always wiser than others. Everywhere they are wiser. They are the magi.

吉姆躺倒在长沙发上，两手放到脑后，笑了。“黛拉，”他说，“咱们还是先把这些礼物收起来吧。它们实在是太好了，咱们现在还不能受用。我把表卖了，给你买的梳子。来吧，咱们吃饭。”

如刚才所说，麦琪是智者，他们非常聪明。他们给初生的耶稣送去了礼物。因为聪明，所以他们送去的礼物也是智慧的礼物。吉姆和黛拉看起来或许并不聪明，他们损失了家里的两件宝物。但是我要告诉你，他们其实很聪明。像吉姆和黛拉这样的人往往比别人聪明——不管在哪儿。因为他们就是麦琪。

---

lie back 休息；放松

wise *adj.* 明智的；聪明的

Love of Life

Adapted from the story by Jack London

Jack London was born in *San Francisco*, in 1876. His family was poor. He left school at fourteen. He worked on boats, on farms, and in the woods. He loved to visit new places. His first long trip was to Japan. When he was eighteen he returned to high school for one year. Then he went to the University of California at Berkeley. But again he left after one year and began to write for money. In 1897 he went to the Klondike, in northwest Canada, near Alaska.

眷恋生命

根据杰克·伦敦的同名故事改写

杰克·伦敦于1876年生于加利福尼亚州的旧金山。他家境贫寒，十四岁时便辍学，在轮船上、农场里、森林里干活。伦敦喜欢游览新地方，第一次长途之旅是去日本。十八岁时，又回到中学就读一年，毕业后上了加州大学伯克利分校。但一年后又弃学，并开始写作。1897年，伦敦去了加拿大北部靠近阿拉斯加的克朗代克河。很多人都去那个寒冷空旷的地方淘金。他写了很多故事，描述那里的经历。还游历过

San Francisco 旧金山（美国城市）

Many men went to find gold in that cold, empty land. London wrote stories about the men and animals there. He traveled to many other different places, too, and found adventures everywhere. He put these adventures into his famous stories and novels. London continued to travel until a few years before his death in 1916.

Two men walked slowly through the low water of a river. They were alone in the cold, empty land. All they could see were stones and earth. It was fall, and the river ran cold over their feet. They carried ***blankets*** on their backs. They had guns, but no ***bullets***; ***matches***, but no food.

"I wish we had just two of those bullets we hid in the ***camp***," said the first of the men. His voice was tired. The other man did not

---

许多不同的地方，所到之处总有一些奇遇。他把这些奇遇统统写进名作之中。他逝世于1916年。在逝世前的几年，他的旅游也一直没有中断。

有两个男人趟着一条浅河慢慢地行走，在这片寒冷而空旷的土地上只有他们两个人，他们所能看到的只有石头和土地。时值秋季，河水冰脚。他们身上背着毯子，有枪，没有子弹；有火柴，没有食物。

"我们要是能把藏在营地里的子弹拿来两颗就好了，"其中一个人说，声音疲惫，另一个人没有作声。

---

blanket *n.* 毛毯
bullet *n.* 子弹
match *n.* 火柴
camp *n.* 营地

answer.

Suddenly the first man fell over a stone. He hurt his foot badly, and he cried out. He lay still for a moment, and then called: "Hey, Bill, I've hurt my foot." Bill didn't stop or look back. He walked out of the river and over the hill. The other man watched him. His eyes seemed like the eyes of a sick animal. He stood up. "Bill!" he cried again. But there was no answer. Bill kept walking.

"Bill!"

The man was alone in the empty land. His hands were cold, and he *dropped* his gun. He fought with his fear, and took his gun out of the water. He *followed* slowly after Bill. He tried to walk lightly on his bad foot.

突然，第一个人被石头绊倒了，脚伤得很厉害，他大声喊叫，一动不动地躺了一会儿，然后高呼："嗨，比尔，我的脚受伤了。"比尔没有停下脚步，也没有回头看看他，径直走出小河，翻过了前面那座山。这个人默默地注视着他，那眼神就像生了病的动物的眼神一样。他站了起来。"比尔！"他又喊道。但仍没有回音。比尔继续往前走。

"比尔！"

旷野里只有他孤零零的一个人。手冰凉，枪也掉落了。他克制着内心的恐惧，从水中拾起枪，慢慢地跟在比尔后面，尽量不让那只受伤的脚吃劲儿。

---

drop *v.* 落下；掉下

follow *v.* 跟着

He was alone, but he was not lost. He knew the way to their camp. There he would find food, bullets, and blankets. He must find them soon. Bill would wait for him there. Together they would go south to the Hudson Bay ***Company***. They would find food there, and a warm fire. Home. The man had to believe that Bill would wait for him at the camp. If not, he would die. He thought about the food in the camp. And the food at the Hudson Bay Company. And the food he ate two days ago. He thought about food and he walked. After a while the man found some small ***berries*** to eat. The berries had no taste, and did not fill him. But he knew he must eat them.

In the evening he hit his foot on a stone and fell down. He could not get up again. He lay still for a long time. Later, he felt a little

他只身一人，但并没有迷路。他知道去营地的路。一到那里，就可以找到食物、子弹和毛毯。他必须尽快找到这些东西，比尔会在那里等他。他们会一同南下去哈得孙湾公司。在那里找到食物，还有温暖的火，还有——家。他必须相信比尔会在营地等他，否则，他就活不下去了。他想起了营地里的食物，想起了哈得孙湾公司的食物，想起了两天前吃过的食物。他一边想着这些食物，一边往前走。过了一会儿，他发现有一些小浆果可以吃。这些小浆果没有什么滋味，也填不饱肚子，但他明白必须把它们吃下去。

傍晚，他一脚磕在石头上，摔倒了。他站不起来，一动不动地躺了很久。后来，感觉稍好一些，就站了起来。他生了一堆火，但只能烧热水，不

company *n.* 公司

berry *n.* 浆果

better and got up. He made a fire. He could cook only hot water, but he felt warmer. He dried his shoes by the fire. They had many ***holes***. His feet had blood on them. His foot hurt badly. He put his foot in a piece of his blanket. Then he slept like a dead man.

He woke up because he heard an animal near him. He thought of meat and took his gun. But he had no bullets. The animal ran away. The man stood up and cried out. His foot was much worse this morning. He took out a small bag that was in his blanket. It was heavy—fifteen ***pounds***. He didn't know if he could carry it. But he couldn't leave it behind. He had to take it with him. He had to be strong enough. He put it into his blanket again.

That day his hunger grew worse, worse than the hurt in his foot.

过，还是感觉暖和了一些。他用火把鞋子烤干，鞋上有很多破洞。他的脚上有血，脚伤很重。他把伤脚伸进一块毯子里，然后就像个死人似的睡过去了。

昏睡中，他听见身旁有动物的声音，便一下子惊醒过来。他想到了动物肉，便一把抓起枪来。可惜没有子弹。那动物逃走了。他站起身来大叫一声。早上起来他的脚伤更严重了。他从毯子里拿出一个小口袋，很沉，有十五磅重。他不知道自己还能不能背得动，但不能把它扔掉，得随身带着，得有足够的力气。他又把口袋放回毯子里。

那天，他的饥饿感加剧了，饥饿的痛苦比起脚痛来更让人难以忍受。有

---

hole *n.* 洞；孔

pound *n.* 英镑

Many times he wanted to lie down, but hunger made him go on. He saw a few birds. Once he tried to catch one, but it flew away. He felt tired and sick. He forgot to follow the way to the camp. In the afternoon he found some green ***plants***. He ate them fast, like a horse. He saw a small fish in a river. He tried to catch it with his cup. But the fish swam away into a hole. The man cried like a baby, first quietly, then loudly. He cried alone in that empty world.

That night he made a fire again, and drank hot water. His blanket was wet, and his foot hurt. He could think only of his hunger. He woke up cold and sick. The earth and sky were ***gray***. He got up and walked, he didn't know where. But the small bag was with him. The sun came out again, and he saw that he was lost. Was he too far

---

好几次他都想倒下去，但辘辘饥肠又迫使他继续前行。他看见几只鸟。有一次，他差点捉住一只，可惜飞走了。他身心疲惫，加上病痛难忍，竟然忘记了走那条回营的路。下午，他发现了一些绿色植物。他像一匹马一样很快就把它们吃掉了。他看到河里有一条小鱼，想用杯子去捞，可是，小鱼一下子钻进洞里不见了。这个大男人像个孩子似的哭了起来。开始时是无声地哭，继而是放声大哭。后来他独自一人在那个空旷的世界里尽情地哭。

当晚他又生了火，喝上了热水。毯子湿漉漉的，脚也很疼。辘辘饥肠搅得他什么心思都没有。一觉醒来，他浑身发冷，他病了。大地和天空都是灰蒙蒙的。他站起来走走，但不知去向，那个小口袋还是带在身上的。太阳又出来了，他看出自己迷了路。是不是太偏北了？他转向东边。饥饿不那么

---

plant *n.* 植物；作物

gray *adj.* 灰色的；苍白的

north? He turned toward the east. His *hunger* was not so great, but he knew he was sick. He stopped often. He heard wolves, and knew that *deer* were near him. He believed he had one more bullet in his gun. But it was still empty. The small bag became too heavy. The man opened the bag. It was full of small pieces of gold. He put half the gold in a piece of his blanket and left it on a rock. But he kept his gun. There were bullets in that camp.

Days passed, days of rain and cold. One day he came to the bones of a deer. There was no meat on the bones. The man knew wolves must be near. He broke the bones and ate like an animal. Would he, too, be only bones tomorrow? And why not? This was life, he thought. Only life hurt. There was no hurt in death. To die was to

---

剧烈了，但他知道自己病了。他时常停下脚步。他听到了狼的声音，知道附近有鹿。他觉得自己的枪膛里还有一发子弹，可结果还是空空如也。那个小口袋越发沉重了。他把它打开，里面满是散碎的金粒。他捧起一半放进毯子里，留在一块岩石上。但那支枪还带着，营地里有子弹。

几天过去了，都是阴冷的雨天。一天，他碰到一堆鹿骨，骨头上没有肉。他知道附近准有狼。他把骨头敲断，像个动物一样猛吃起来。到明天，他也只能变成一堆白骨吗？为什么不会呢？他觉得这就是生活。只有活着才能感受疼痛，死了就再也感受不到了。死亡就如同睡眠。那么，他为什么就

---

hunger *n.* 饿；饥饿

deer *n.* 鹿

sleep. Then why was he not ready to die? He could not see or feel. The hunger, too, was gone. But he walked and walked.

One morning he woke up beside a river. ***Sunlight*** was warm on his face. A sunny day, he thought. Perhaps he could find his way to the camp. His eyes followed the river. He could see far. The river emptied into the sea. He saw a ship on that ***silver*** sea. He shut his eyes. He knew there could be no ship, no seas, in this land. He heard a noise behind him, and turned back. A wolf, old and sick, was following him. I know this is real, he thought. He turned again, but the sea and the ship were still there. He didn't understand it. He tried to remember. What did the men at the Hudson Bay Company say about this land? Was he walking north, away from the camp,

---

不想死呢？他现在既看不到，也感觉不到，连饥饿感也消失了，但他仍在不停地走。

一天早晨，他在河边醒来，阳光暖暖地照在他脸上。这是个晴天。他想，说不定能找到回营地的路呢。他顺着河水望去，能望出很远。河水流进了大海。在银色的海面上有一艘轮船。他闭上了眼睛，知道在这个地方不会有轮船，不会有大海。他听到背后有声音，便转过身来，是一只狼，病老不堪，正跟着他。他心里想，这回可不是虚幻。他又转过身来，大海和轮船仍在。他闹不明白了。他极力回想，哈得孙湾的人对这个地方是怎么说的了？他这是在向北走，离开了营地的方向，是在朝大海走吗？他慢慢地向那条船

---

sunlight *n.* 日光

silver *adj.* 银色的；银白色的

toward the sea? The man moved slowly toward the ship. He knew the sick wolf was following him. In the afternoon, he found more bones left by ***wolves***. The bones of a man! Beside the bones was a small bag of gold, like his own. Ha! Bill carried his gold to the end, he thought. He would take Bill's gold to the ship. He would have the last laugh on Bill. His laughing sounded like the low cry of an animal. The wolf cried back to the man, and the man stopped laughing. How could he laugh about Bill's bones? He could not take Bill's gold. He left the gold near the bones.

The man was very sick now. He walked more and more slowly. His blanket was gone. He lost his gold, then his gun, then his knife. Only the wolf stayed with him hour after hour. At last the man could

---

挪动脚步。他知道那只病狼在跟着他。下午，他又发现一些狼吃剩的骨头，这回是人骨！骨头旁边有一小袋金子，和他自己的一样。哈！他想，比尔到死还带着金子。他可以把比尔的金子带上船，可以给比尔最后的嘲笑。他的笑声就像动物的低吼，那只狼也回应了一声，他便止住不笑了。他怎么能嘲笑比尔的白骨呢？不能拿比尔的金子，他把金子留在那些白骨旁边。

这人现在病得很重，走路也越来越慢了。他的毯子没了，金子也丢了，后来枪又丢了，再后来刀也没了，只剩下那只狼一直跟着他。最后，他一步

---

toward *prep.* 向；朝着

wolf *n.* 狼

go no further. He fell down. The wolf came close to him. It weakly ***bit*** his hand. The man hit the wolf and it went away. But it did not go far. It waited. The man waited. After many hours the wolf came back again. It was going to kill the man. But the man was ready. He held the wolf's mouth closed, and he got on top of the sick wolf. He held the animal still. Then he bit it with his last ***strength***. He tasted the wolf's blood in his mouth. Only love of life gave him enough strength. He held the wolf with his ***teeth*** and killed it. Later he fell on his back and slept.

The men on the ship saw a strange thing on the land. It did not walk. It was lying on the ground, and it moved slowly toward them—

也走不动了，一头跌倒在地。那只狼跟了上来，虚弱地咬了咬他的手。他挥手打了狼一下，狼躲开了，但没走多远。狼在等候时机，他也在等候时机。过了很久，那狼又回来了，想对他下手。但他早有准备，他捏住狼嘴不让它张开，又骑到病狼的背上，把它按住不动，然后使出最后的力气咬它。他尝到了狼血的滋味。对生命的热爱给了他足够的力量。他用牙齿紧紧地咬住狼，把它咬死了。随后他仰面摔倒在地，睡过去了。

船上的人看到陆地上有个奇怪的东西，它不走，躺在地上，而且还缓慢地向他们移近——大约一小时能移动20英尺。他们走近一看，简直不敢相信那居然是一个人。

---

bite *v.* 咬疼；咬伤

strength *n.* 力量；力气

tooth *n.* 牙齿

perhaps twenty feet an hour. The men went close to look at it. They could not ***believe*** it was a man.

Three weeks later the man felt *better.* He could tell them his story. But there was one strange thing. He could not believe there was enough food on the ship. The men told him there was a lot of food. But he only looked at them with ***fear***. And slowly he began to grow fat. The men thought this was strange. They gave him less food, but still he grew larger and larger—each day he was fatter. Then one day they saw him put a lot of bread under his shirt. They looked in his bed, too, and saw bread under his blanket. The men understood, and left him alone.

三个星期后，这人感觉好多了，可以讲述自己的经历了。可是有一件事很奇怪：他无法相信船上有足够的食物。人们告诉他船上的食物多得很，可他只是用恐惧的目光看着他们。慢慢地，他开始发胖。他们觉得奇怪，就少给一些吃的，可他还是越来越胖——每天都在长胖。后来有一天，他们看到他把很多面包藏到衬衫底下。又查看了他的床铺，看到在毛毯下面也有面包。他们什么都明白了，也就随他的便了。

---

believe *v.* 相信

fear *n.* 恐惧

The Tell-Tale Heart

Adapted from the story by Edgar Allan Poe

Edgar Allan Poe was born in 1809 in Boston, Massachusetts. Poe's parents died when he was a little child. After that, he lived with a family named Allan. They moved to England for five years when Poe was six. Although he was an ***excellent*** student and swimmer as a boy and young man, Poe led a very unhappy, troubled life. He often fought with Mr. Allan, and finally ***separated*** from him at the age of twenty-two. Allan had become very rich, but Poe was

泄密的心

根据艾德加·艾伦·坡的同名故事改编

艾德加·爱伦·坡1809年生于马萨诸塞州的波士顿。父母早在他儿时就去世了。他跟爱伦一家生活。坡6岁时举家移居英格兰。在那里待了5年。他幼年学习很好，长大后在游泳方面很擅长，但是过着窘迫且不快乐的生活。他经常与爱伦先生吵架，22岁时离家出走。爱伦先生很富有，但坡却一直到生命的最后还很贫穷。他曾为一些杂志社工

excellent *adj.* 杰出的；优秀的

separate *v.* 分开；离开

The Tell-Tale Heart

poor for the rest of his life. He worked for magazines, but drank too much and lost many jobs. He married his young cousin, Virginia, but she became sick and died. Through all his difficulties, Poe never stopped writing, and his writing took many ***forms***. He often wrote about the dark side of the human heart. He was interested in what lies between the real and the unreal in our lives. People remember Poe now for his ***poetry*** and for his dark, strange stories like "The Tell-Tale Heart." Poe died at the age of forty in 1849.

True! Nervous. I was nervous then and I am nervous now. But why do you say that I am mad? Nothing was wrong with me. I could see very well. I could smell. I could touch. Yes, my friend, and I could hear. I could hear all things in the skies and in the earth. So why do you think that I am mad? Listen. I will tell you the story. I will speak

---

作，但因经常酗酒多次失业。他娶了自己年轻的表妹弗吉尼亚，但她后来病故了。坡经历了重重困难，但从未停止过写作。他的作品体裁多样，经常描写人类灵魂的阴暗面。他对生活中真实或不真实的谎言很感兴趣。人们至今仍记得他的诗和"泄密的心"之类阴森、怪诞的故事。坡于1849年逝世，年仅40岁。

的确！很紧张。我当时很紧张，现在也很紧张。可你为什么说我疯了？我什么毛病都没有。我的视觉非常清晰。我的嗅觉灵敏，触觉正常。是的，朋友，我的听觉也没问题。我能听得见天上地上所有的声音。可你为什么认为我疯了？听着，我要把整件事和盘托出。我要心平气和地讲给你听，你听

---

form *n.* 形式　　　　poetry *n.* 诗；诗歌

quietly. You will understand everything. Listen!

Why did I want to kill the old man? Ah, this is very difficult. I liked the old man. No, I loved him! He never hurt me. He was always kind to me. I didn't need his gold; no, I didn't want that. I think it was his eye—yes, it was this! He had the eye of a bird. It was a cold, light-blue eye—a ***horrible*** eye. I feared it. Sometimes I tried to look at it. But then my blood ran cold. So, after many weeks, I knew I must kill the old man. His horrible eye must not live. Do you understand?

Now here is the point. You think that I am mad. ***Madmen*** know nothing. But I? I was careful. Oh, I was very careful. Careful, you see? For one long week, I was very kind to the old man. But every night, at midnight, I opened his door slowly, carefully. I had a ***lantern*** with me. Inside the lantern there was a light. But the sides of the

---

完就什么都明白了。现在你听好了！

我当初为什么要杀那个老头儿？哈，这可真难说。我喜欢他，不，是爱他！他从不伤害我，一直对我很好。我不需要他的金钱，不，我不想要。我猜是他的眼睛——对，就是他的眼睛！他长着一双鸟眼，那是一双冷冰冰的、淡蓝色的眼睛，是一双可怕的眼睛。我害怕这双眼睛。有时我试图看着它们，可一到这时我的血液就变得冰冷。所以，几个星期过后，我就知道我必须干掉这老头儿。他那双可怕的眼睛绝不能活下去，你明白吗？

好了，现在的问题是：你认为我疯了，可疯子是什么都不知道的。而我呢？我却很谨慎。哦，我非常谨慎。“谨慎”，你懂吗？在那漫长的一星期里，我对那老头儿非常好。但是每天晚上，到了半夜，我就慢慢地、小心地

---

horrible *adj.* 可怕的；恐怖的　　madman *n.* 疯子；狂人

lantern *n.* 灯笼；提灯

lantern hid the light. So, first I put the dark lantern through the open door. Then I put my head in the room. I put it in slowly, very slowly. I didn't want to wake the old man. Ha! Would a madman be ***careful***, like that? There was no noise, not a sound. I opened the lantern carefully—very carefully—and slowly. A thin light fell upon the old man's eye. I held it there. I held it there for a long time. And I did this every night for seven nights. But always the eye was closed. And so I could not do my work. I was not angry at the old man, you see. I was angry only at his horrible eye. And every morning I went into his room ***happily***. I was friendly with him. I asked about his night. Did he sleep well? Was he all right? And so, you see, he knew nothing.

On the eighth night, I was more careful than before. I know you don't believe me, but it is true. The clock's ***hand*** moved more

---

打开他的房门。我带着一个灯笼，灯笼里有光，但被我遮住了。我先把这个遮了光的灯笼从门缝里探进去，然后再向屋里探头，我一点一点地向里探，动作非常非常缓慢。我不想把老头儿惊醒。哈！疯子懂得这么小心吗？没有动静，一点声音也没有。我小心地揭开灯笼的遮盖——非常小心——也非常缓慢。一缕微光照在老头儿的眼睛上。我举着灯笼，就那样举了很久。我每天晚上都这么干，一连干了七个晚上。但那双眼睛总是闭着，所以我就没法下手。你知道，我并不生老头儿的气，只是生他那双可怕的眼睛的气。每天早晨我都愉快地走进他的房间。我跟他很友好，问他夜间的情况，问他睡得好不好，感觉怎么样。所以，你看，他一无所知。

第八个夜晚，我比以往更谨慎。我知道你不相信，但这是事实。我手的

---

careful *adj.* 仔细的；小心的

happily *adv.* 快乐地

hand *n.* 指针

quickly than my hand. I opened the door slowly. I put the lantern in the room. The old man moved suddenly in his bed. But I did not go back. The room was very dark. I knew he could not see me. I put my head in the room. I began to open the lantern, but my hand hit the side. It made a loud noise.

The old man sat up quickly in bed. "Who's there?" he cried.

I stood still and said nothing. For one long hour I did not move a ***finger***. And he did not lie down. He sat in his bed. He listened. I knew his fear!

And soon I heard another sound. It came from the old man. It was a horrible sound, the sound of fear! I knew that sound well. Often, at night, I too have made that sound. What was in the room? The old man didn't know. He didn't want to know. But he knew that he was ***in danger***. Ah, yes, he knew!

动作比钟表的指针还要慢。我慢慢地打开门，把灯笼伸进屋里。老头突然在床上动了一下，但我并没有后退。屋里漆黑一片。我知道他看不见我。我把头探了进去，又去掀灯笼的遮盖，但手碰到了侧壁，弄出很大的响声。

老头儿忽地坐了起来。"谁？"他大喊一声。

我站着不动，一声不吭。足足有一个小时，我连手指都没动一下，他也没有躺下。他就坐在床上，倾听着。我知道他害怕！

不久，我就听到了另一种声音，是那老头儿发出来的。那是一种可怕的声音，是因为恐惧而发出的声音！我很熟悉这种声音。因为，经常地，在夜间，我也发出这种声音。屋里有什么？老头儿不知道。他也不想知道，但他知道自己正处于危险之中。哈，是的，他知道！

---

finger *n.* 手指　　　　**in danger** 处于危险之中

And now I began to open the lantern. I opened it just a little. A small thin light fell upon the horrible blue eye.

It was open—wide, wide open. I could not see the old man's face or body. But I saw the eye very well. The horrible bird's eye. My blood ran cold. At the same time, anger began to grow inside me.

And now, haven't told you that I could hear everything? Now a low, quick sound came to my ears. It was like the sound of a small wooden clock. I knew that sound well, too. It was the beating of the old man's heart!

My fear and anger grew. But I did not move. I stood still. I held the light on the old man's eye. And the beating of the heart grew. It became quicker and quicker, and louder and louder every ***second***! I knew that his fear was very great. Louder, do you hear? I have told you that I am ***nervous***. And this is true. My fear was like the old

---

我又开始掀灯笼遮盖，只掀开一点儿，一小束微光照到了那双可怕的蓝眼睛上。

眼睛睁开了——睁得很大，很大。我看不见老头儿的面孔，也看不见他的身体，但我能清清楚楚地看见他的眼睛，那双可怕的鸟眼。我的血液开始冷却，我心中的愤怒也随之增加。

我不是告诉过你我什么都能听见吗？这会儿，一种低低的、急促的声音传到我的耳鼓，很像一座小木钟发出的声音。这种声音我也很熟悉，是老头儿的心在狂跳！

我越来越害怕，也越来越生气。但我一动也不动，就那么站着。我把光照在老头儿的眼睛上。他的心跳加剧了，每秒钟都在加快，而且越来越响。我知道他极为恐惧。他心跳的声音更大了，你听见了吗？我对你说过我很紧张，

---

second *n.* 秒　　nervous *adj.* 紧张不安的

man's. But I did not move. I held the light on his eye. But the beating grew louder, LOUDER! And now a new fear came to me. Someone in the next house would hear! The old man must die! This was his hour! With a loud cry, I opened the lantern wide. I ran into the room! The old man cried loudly once—once only. His fear, his fear killed him! ***In a second*** I pulled him from the bed. He lay still. I smiled a little. Everything was all right. For some minutes, I heard his heart beat ***softly***. Then it stopped. I put my hand on his body. He was cold. He was like a stone. The old man was dead. His eye would never look upon me again!

And now I was very, very careful. I worked quickly but quietly. I

这是真的。我跟老头儿一样恐惧，但我没动。我把灯光照在他的眼睛上。他的心跳得越来越响，越来越响！这会儿，一种新的恐惧又袭上我的心头：隔壁会有人听见的！老头儿必死无疑！他的时辰已到！我大叫一声，掀开灯笼，冲进屋去！老头惨叫一声——只一声。他的恐惧，是他的恐惧要了他的命！我立即把他从床上拖下来。他一动不动。我笑了笑，一切顺利。有那么几分钟，我听见他心脏还在轻微地跳动，然后就停下了。我用手试试他的身体，凉了，像块石头。老头儿死了，他的目光再也不会落到我的身上了。

这会儿，我是非常、非常谨小慎微。我干得很快，但却没有一点儿声

---

in a second 立刻；很快

softly *adv.* 轻轻地

used a good, new knife. I ***cut off*** the old man's arms and legs and head. Then I took three boards from the floor of the room. I put everything below the floor. Then I put the boards in their place again. I cleaned the floor. There was no blood. Nothing was wrong. I was careful, you see? Ha! Can you still think that I am mad?

I finished. It was four o'clock—still dark as ***midnight***. Suddenly there was a beating on the door. Someone was there. But I went down with a happy heart. I had nothing to fear. Nothing.

Three policemen came into the house. They said that someone in the next house heard a cry. Was something wrong? Was everyone all right?

音。我用一把锋利的新刀把他的四肢和头都切了下来。然后撬开三块屋内的地板，把碎尸放了进去，再把地板块归位。我把地板擦净，一丝血迹也没有留下。没有任何破绽。你看到了吧，我是非常谨慎的。哈，你还认为我疯了吗?

这一切都干完了，时间是凌晨四点，天还和午夜时一样漆黑。突然，有敲门声，是什么人来了。但我心情愉快地过去开门。我没有什么可害怕的。一点儿也没有。

三个警察走了进来。他们说隔壁有人听见一声叫喊，问出了什么事没有，是不是每个人都好。

---

cut off 切掉；割掉

midnight *n.* 午夜；半夜12点钟

"Of course," I said. "Please come in." I was not nervous. I smiled at the men. I told them that the old man was in another town. I said he was with his sister. I showed them his money, his gold. Everything was there, in its place.

I brought chairs. I asked the men to sit. I sat, too. I sat on the ***boards*** over the dead man's body! I talked easily. The policemen smiled.

But after some minutes I became tired. Perhaps I was a little nervous. There was a low sound in my head, in my ears. I didn't like it. I talked more ***loudly***, more angrily. Then suddenly I understood. The sound was not in my head or in my ears. It was there in the

---

"当然"，我说。"请进吧"。我并不紧张，我对他们笑脸相迎。我对他们说老头儿到别的城里去了，他现在正跟他妹妹在一起。我还把他的钱，他的金子，统统拿给他们看，一切都在，完好无损。

我搬来椅子，请警察们坐下，我也坐下了。我就坐在尸体上面的地板上！我的谈吐轻松自如，警察们笑了。

但几分钟后我就觉得很疲惫。也许是有些紧张。我的脑海里、耳朵里出现了一种低沉的声音。我不喜欢这种声音。于是，我就使劲地说话，生气地说话。突然，我一下子明白了，那声音不在我脑袋里，也不在我耳朵里，而

---

board *n.* 木板　　loudly *adv.* 大声地

room!

Now I know that I became very nervous. It was a low, quick sound. It sounded like a small wooden clock! My eyes opened wide. Could the policemen hear it? I talked in a louder voice. But the noise did not stop. It grew! I stood up and talked angrily, dangerously. I walked across the floor and back again. Why wouldn't the men leave? There was a ***storm*** inside my head! And still the noise became louder—LOUDER—LOUDER! I beat my hands on the table. I said dangerous things in a loud voice. But still the men talked happily and smiled. Couldn't they hear? Was it possible? Oh, God! No, no! They heard! They knew! They ***laughed at*** my hopes, and smiled at my

---

是在屋子里！

这下我知道自己已经是非常紧张了。这是一种低沉的、急促的声音，听起来像个小木钟！我瞪大了双眼。警察能听见这声音吗？我又加大了说话的音量，但噪音不仅没有停下来，反倒越来越响了！我站起身来，气愤地、威胁地说着，在地板上来回走动。这些人怎么不走啊？我的脑袋里刮起了风暴！而且那声音越来越响——越来越响——越来越响！我用双手拍桌子，大声地说些危险的事情，可他们仍旧谈笑风生。难道他们听不见吗？有这种可能吗？哦，上帝！不，不！他们听得见！他们知道了！他们在嘲笑我的希

---

storm *n.* 暴风雨；风暴

laugh at 嘲笑；讥笑

fears. I knew it then and I know it now. I couldn't keep still! Anything was better than their smiles and laughing! And now—again—listen! louder! LOUDER! LOUDER!

"Stop!" I cried. "Enough! Enough! ***Pull up*** the boards! Below the floor! Here, here—It is the beating of his horrible heart!"

望，嘲笑我的恐惧。我当时就知道，我现在也明白。我不可能无动于衷！没有什么能比他们的笑，不管是微笑，还是嘲笑更糟糕的了！你瞧——又来了！——你听！更响了！越来越响！越来越响！

“住嘴！”我大叫起来。“够了！够了！把地板掀开！就在地板下面！在这儿，在这儿！——是老头儿那可怕的心脏在跳！”

---

pull up 把……向上拉

Of the Coming of John

Adapted from the story by W.E.B Du Bois

W. E. B. Du Bois (pronounced Do-BOYS) was born in 1868 in Great Barrington, Massachusetts. He was the only black student in his class at school. He was an excellent student and began to write for a black *newspaper* when he was fifteen. He went to Fisk University, a *college* for black students in Nashville, Tennessee. He later wrote that those first years in the South were difficult for him. He felt that it was even harder in the South than in the North for

---

约翰的归来

根据杜·博伊斯的同名故事改写

W. E. B. 杜·博伊斯1868 年生于马萨诸塞州的大巴灵顿。小学时，他是班里唯一的黑人学生。他成绩优异，15岁就开始给一家黑人报纸撰稿。就读的菲斯克大学是一所黑人学校，坐落于田纳西州的纳什维尔。他后来写道，在南方的最初几年是很艰难的。在那个所有权力都属于白人的世界里，黑人的日子在南方比在北方更难熬。杜·博伊斯

---

newspaper *n.* 报纸　　college *n.* 大学；学院

Of the Coming of John

black people to live in a world where whites had all the power. Du Bois later studied at the University of Berlin in Germany, and he was the first African American to earn a Ph.D. from Harvard University. Later he taught at Atlanta University, and also lived and worked in New York City. When he was ninety-three, he decided he could live no longer in the United States where he had found it impossible to turn his ***beliefs*** into reality. He moved to Ghana, in Africa, in 1961, and died two years later. "Of the Coming of John" is from his most famous book, *The Souls of Black Folk* (1903).

I

The bell rings at Wells ***Institute***, and the students come in for supper. Tall and black, they move slowly, like ***ghosts*** against the light of ***sunset***. Perhaps they are ghosts here. For this is a college for

---

后来去了德国的柏林大学。他是第一个在哈佛大学得到博士学位的非裔美国人。后来，他曾执教于亚特兰大大学，也在纽约市生活和工作过。93岁时，他决定离开美国，因为他意识到在那里不可能把理想变为现实。1961年，他移居非洲的加纳。两年后辞世。"约翰的归来"选自他的代表作《黑人的灵魂》（1903）。

I

威尔士学院的铃声响了，学生们都进来吃饭。他们又高又黑，排着队慢慢往前走，在落日的辉映下，一个个都像黑鬼。也许他们就是这里的鬼，因为这是在白人市区外的一所黑人学校。这些学生几乎从不进市区。在白人眼里，他们简直就不存在。

---

belief *n.* 信念；信仰
ghost *n.* 鬼；幽灵
institute *n.* 学院
sunset *n.* 日落

black students outside of a white city. The students almost never go into the city. The students almost don't *exist* for the whites.

Every evening, there is one student who always runs in late. The other students laugh as John hurries in after the bell. At first, his teachers excuse his *lateness*. He is a tall, thin brown boy. He seems to be growing out of his clothes. He is young and thoughtless. But he has a nice smile. He seems happy with the world.

John Jones came to Wells Institute from Altamaha in southeast Georgia. The white people of Altamaha thought John was a good boy. He was a good farm worker. And he was always smiling and *respectful*. But they shook their heads in wonder when his mother sent him north to college. The white *mailman* said what most of the white people thought. "It will spoil him—destroy him," he said

---

每天傍晚，总有一个学生迟到。他叫约翰，在响铃之后才匆匆进来，同学都取笑他。起初，老师们还能原谅他。他又高又瘦的，棕色皮肤，由于发育过快身上的衣服已经明显不相称了。他还年轻，做事欠考虑，但他笑起来很好看，好像对这个世界挺心满意足。

约翰·琼斯是从佐治亚州东南部的阿尔塔玛哈来威尔士学院的。阿尔塔玛哈的白人认为约翰是个好孩子。他在农场手脚勤快，又总是面带微笑，对人也很礼貌。可是，当母亲送他到北方上大学时，他们都疑惑地摇头。那个白人邮差说出了多数白人的想法："那会害了他，会把他给毁了，"他认真地说。他说这话就好像他肯定知道似的。

---

exist *v.* 存在

lateness *n.* 晚；迟

respectful *adj.* 恭敬的

mailman *n.* 邮差；邮递员

seriously. And he spoke as if he knew.

But on the day John left for college, half the black folk in town followed him to the train. They were so proud of him. The girls kissed him goodbye. The boys laughed and shook his hand. The train ***whistled***. It was time to go. He kissed his little sister. He threw his long arms around his mother. The train whistled again, and carried him north, through the fields and farms, to Wells Institute.

John was their friend, brother, and son. After he left, his people kept saying ***proudly***, "When John comes..." So many things would happen when John came home. Parties, speaking in ***church***. John would learn to be a teacher, and there would be a new schoolhouse. They had so many hopes for how John would help them. "When John comes..." But the white people wondered. They shook their

---

可是，就在约翰要上大学的那天，城里有一半的人都跟着去了火车站。他们为约翰而自豪。姑娘们与他吻别，小伙子们欢笑着与他握手告别。列车拉响了汽笛，离别的时间到了。他吻了吻小妹，又张开长臂拥抱一下母亲。随着又一次鸣笛，列车徐徐开往北方，穿过无数田野和农场，最终把他带到威尔士学院。

约翰是他们的朋友，兄弟，儿子。他走后，乡亲们总是自豪地说："等约翰回来……"他们的意思是，等约翰回来后就会有那么多的事情要发生，有舞会，有教堂里的演说。约翰还得学会当老师，还得筹建一所新学校。他们有那么多的希望，都在等着约翰回来帮助他们实现。"等约翰回来……"但那些白人却持怀疑态度，他们摇着头说："学校会把他给毁了的。"

---

seriously *adv.* 认真地；严肃地

proudly *adv.* 傲慢地

whistle *v.* 鸣汽笛

church *n.* 教堂

heads. "School will spoil him."

At first, John was going to come home at Christmas. But the *vacation* was too short. Then for the summer. But his mother was poor, and the school cost a lot. So he worked at the Institute instead. Time went by, and two years passed. John's friends grew up, and his mother grew gray. His little sister, Jennie, went to work in a white man's kitchen. This man was a *judge*, rich and important.

Up at the Judge's house, the white people liked to hear the blacks say, "When John comes..." The Judge and his wife had a son named John, too. Their son John was tall and blond. When they were little, the two Johns had sometimes played together. Now he was away at college, too. At Princeton University. His parents were very proud of him. "He'll show those Northerners what a Southern

---

起初，约翰打算圣诞节回家，可假期太短，又推到暑期。然而，那时又因为家里很穷，学校的费用很高，就只好在学校打工了。时光飞逝，转眼两年过去了。约翰的朋友们都已长大成人，他的母亲也变得白发苍苍，小妹珍妮去给一户白人家当厨房女佣。这家主人是个法官，有钱有势。

在高高在上的法官家里，那些白人喜欢听黑人说"等约翰回来……"这句话。法官夫妇有个儿子，也叫约翰。他们的约翰是高高的金发男孩。两个约翰小时候时常在一起玩。如今，这个约翰也上大学了，在普林斯顿大学就读。他的父母非常骄傲。那法官总是自豪地说"他会让那些北方人看看，一

---

vacation *n.* 假期；休假

judge *n.* 法官

gentleman can do!" the Judge would say proudly. And then he would say to Jennie, "How's your John? Too bad your mother sent him away to school. It will ***spoil*** him." He shook his head. Jennie listened to him ***respectfully***. And she wondered.

II

Up at Wells Institute, John's teachers were seriously worried about him. He was loud and noisy, always laughing and singing. He didn't know how to study. He seemed bored by books, and his schoolwork was careless. He was always late for everything. One night his teachers met together to ***discuss*** him. They decided "that John Jones, because of ***continual*** lateness and careless work, must leave Wells Institute." Now John understood for the first time that

---

个南方绅士都能干些什么！"他还会问珍妮"你们家的约翰怎么样了？你妈送他上大学可实在是太糟糕了，这肯定得毁了他。"说着，还摇摇头。珍妮恭敬地听着，心里也很疑惑。

II

在北方的威尔士学院里，约翰的老师都非常担心他的情况。他总是大声喧哗，不是哈哈大笑，就是放声歌唱。他不会学习，好像厌倦书本，对学业毫不在乎，做什么事都拖拖拉拉。一天晚上，老师们聚在一起讨论他的问题，最后做出如下决定："鉴于约翰·琼斯频频迟到，不认真学习，威尔士学院决定将其开除。"至此，约翰才生平第一次懂得了学校的重要性。他终

---

spoil *v.* 毁掉
respectfully *adv.* 尊敬地
discuss *v.* 讨论
continual *adj.* 持续不断的

school was really important. He understood at last that his noise and *carelessness* and continual lateness had got him into serious trouble with his teachers.

"But don't tell Mammy—you won't write to my mother, will you?" he said. "If you don't tell her, I'll go into the city and work. And I'll come back next fall and show you something." His teachers liked him. They wanted to help him. They *agreed* that he could come back in the fall and try again.

It seemed to his teachers that John's face was always serious after that. When he returned to the Institute he began to respect his *education*, and he worked hard. He grew in body as well as mind. Slowly his clothes began to *fit* him better. His shirts were clean

---

于明白了自己的吵闹声，对什么事都漫不经心，加上屡屡迟到给老师惹来的严重麻烦。

“但别告诉我母亲——你们不会给她写信的，是吧？”他说。“如果你们不告诉她，我就去市里找工作，明年秋天再回来让你们看看。”老师们还是喜欢他的，也想帮他，于是，就同意让他秋天再回来试试。

从那以后，老师们觉得约翰的面容一直很严肃。返校后他开始注重学习，也很努力。他的身心都在成长。逐渐地，他的衣着开始得体，衬衫干净，皮鞋光亮。随着岁月的流逝，他变得善于思考了。老师们亲眼看见这个不拘小节的男孩变成一个严肃的男人。

---

carelessness *n.* 粗心大意
education *n.* 教育
agree *v.* 同意
fit *v.* 适合；符合

and his shoes were shiny. As the days passed he became more ***thoughtful***. His teachers began to see that this careless boy was becoming a ***serious*** man.

Now John began to look at the world around him. He began to notice the difference between the lives of blacks and whites. He became angry when whites spoke to him without respect. Because he felt like a ghost in their world, he spent long hours worrying about the color line.

III

At last the day came when John finished Wells Institute. It was time to go back to Altamaha. He had always planned to work there after college. But now he wondered about living in that small town. Altamaha was deep in the South. Life wasn't easy for colored folk

---

现在，约翰开始观察他身边的世界。他注意到白人和黑人生活的差别。当白人粗鲁地跟他说话时，他很恼火，感到在他们的世界里自己就是一个鬼。他长时间忧虑着种族间的界线问题。

III

终于有一天，约翰完成了威尔士学院的学业，该回阿尔塔玛哈了。他一直打算毕业后回家乡工作。而如今，他对生活在那个小城镇有些犹豫了。阿尔塔玛哈位于南方腹地。虽说黑人在北方的日子不好过，可在南方更难。约

---

thoughtful *adj.* 沉思的；思考的

serious *adj.* 严肃的；严重的

in the North, but it was even harder in the South. John knew he had to go back home. But he needed to take some time for himself first. So he decided to visit New York City first. "A breath of northern air before I go down South," he told himself.

It was a bright morning in September. John sat watching the people walk by on the New York streets. He looked at all the rich clothes, the ***fashionable*** hats. "This is the big world, the real world," he thought.

He saw a lot of people going into a ***grand*** building. He was interested, and wondered what they were going to see. When he saw a tall blond man and a fashionably dressed woman go inside, he decided to follow.

Inside, John found himself in a line to buy ***tickets***. He wasn't sure

---

翰明白他必须回家，但他需要一些时间作好思想准备。于是，他便决定先去纽约看看。他对自己说："南下前再呼吸一次北方的空气。"

九月，一个晴朗的早晨，约翰坐在那里观看纽约市大街上的过往行人。他看到那些华丽的衣服，时髦的帽子，心想："这就是大千世界，真实的世界。"

他看到有很多人走进了一幢大楼里，觉得很好奇，不知他们要去看什么。当他看到一个高个儿的金发男子和一位衣着时尚的女士走进去时，他便决定跟上他们。

进了楼，他发觉自己也跟着站到了排队买票的队伍中，不知如何是好。

---

fashionable *adj.* 流行的；时髦的　　**grand** *adj.* （建筑物等）庄严的；壮丽的

ticket *n.* 票；入场券

what to do. He had very little money. But he pulled out a five-dollar ***bill*** he had carefully saved. He was very surprised when he got no change back. How could he spend so much money on—what?

John began to hear soft voices behind him. "***Be careful***," he heard a woman say. She seemed to be joking with the man beside her. "You mustn't get angry just because a black man is in front of you in line."

"You don't understand us Southerners," said the blond man beside her. "You say there's no color line in the North. But we're more friendly to colored folk than you are. Why, my best friend when I was a boy was black. He was named John after me. We're friendly, but we don't spoil them, there."

They all sat down in the large music ***hall***. In front of them,

---

他没有什么钱，但还是忍痛抽出自己悉心积攒的五元钞票。五元钱居然没有找零，这使他非常震惊。他怎么能花这么多钱来买——什么？

这时，约翰听到身后传来了温柔的说话声：“当心点儿，”是个女人在说话。她好像在和她身边的男人开玩笑。“你可别因为前面站着个黑人就生气。”

“你不了解我们南方人，”他旁边的金发男子说。“你说北方没有种族界线。而我们南方人对待黑人更友好。我小时候有个最好的朋友就是黑人，他随我起的名，也叫约翰。我们的关系不错，但是，在南方我们并不伤害他们。”

他们都在一个大音乐厅里坐下来。前面的音乐家和歌手已经准备就绪。

---

bill *n.* 钞票

be careful 小心；当心

hall *n.* 大厅；礼堂

musicians and singers were ready to begin. The blond man looked angry when he saw that John was sitting beside them. But John didn't ***notice***. He was too busy looking around. The inside of the building was beautiful. This was a world so different from his! Then the singing began. John felt that he was in a dream. He closed his eyes. The beautiful music rose up in the air. He wanted so much to rise up with it. He wanted to leave his low life. To fly like a bird in the free, sweet air. To live with pride in a world of beauty, and to feel that others respected him. As John sat forward to listen, his arm touched the lady next to him. The blond man noticed, and his face grew red. He lifted his arm to call someone.

John was ***completely*** lost in the music. At first he didn't hear the ***usher***.

金发男子看到约翰坐在他们旁边非常生气。但约翰并没有注意，他正忙着环顾四周。楼内的装修很漂亮。这是一个完全不同的世界。这时，演唱开始了，约翰觉得自己恍若入了梦境。他闭上眼睛，美妙的乐声在空中缭绕，他多想随着音乐一起升空啊！他想脱离他那低微的生活，在自由、芳香的空气中像鸟儿一样飞翔，在一个美丽的世界里骄傲地活着，去感受别人的尊重。就在约翰探身倾听时，他的胳膊无意间碰到了身旁的女士。金发男子看见了，气得面红耳赤，举起手臂唤人过来。

约翰完全沉浸在音乐中，起初并没有听见领座员对他说话。

---

musician *n.* 音乐家
notice *v.* 注意到
completely *adv.* 完全地；彻底地
usher *n.* 引座员；带位员

"Please come with me, sir," the usher said softly. John was surprised.

As he stood up, he saw the angry face of the blond man for the first time. The man ***recognized*** John. And John saw that the man was the Judge's son.

"I'm sorry sir," the usher said when they had left the music hall. "We gave you the wrong seat. That seat was already sold. I am so sorry. Of course, we will give you back your money..."

But John turned and walked out of the building. "You're such a fool, John," he said, now angry at himself. He walked to his ***hotel*** and wrote a letter. "Dear mother and sister—I am coming—John."

IV

Down in Altamaha, all the world knew John was coming. Most

"请跟我来，先生。"领座员轻轻地说。约翰吃了一惊。

就在起身时，他才第一次看到金发男子那愤怒的面孔。那人认出了约翰，约翰也看出他就是法官的儿子。

"对不起，先生，"出了音乐厅，领座员说。"我们把座位安排错了，您的座位已经售出。非常抱歉。当然，我们会把钱返还给您……"

然而约翰却转身走出那幢大楼。"约翰，你可真是个大傻瓜，"他生气地对自己说。他走回旅馆，写了封信。"亲爱的妈妈和小妹——我要回来了——约翰。"

IV

在南方的阿尔塔玛哈，所有人都知道约翰要回来了。多数黑人同胞都

---

recognize *v.* 认出　　hotel *n.* 旅馆；饭店

of the black folk came to meet his train. They were proud and ***excited***. "John's coming!" they called to each other. They talked about the party for John at the church that night. They laughed and listened for the whistle of the train.

But John felt ***unhappy*** as he got off the train and looked around him. He was already angry because he had to ride south in a train car for blacks only. Now, the small, dirty town, the colorful, ***dirty*** faces of his people, made him sad. He had little to say to the happy group who came to welcome him. And the people quickly began to wonder about him. Was this cold, silent man their John? They had waited so long for him to come. Where was his smile, his laughter, his friendly ***handshake***?

来接站。他们感到自豪和兴奋。“约翰要回来啦！”他们奔走相告，谈论着当晚要在教堂为约翰举办的晚会。他们在欢笑声中企盼着约翰的火车呼啸而归。

然而，约翰走下火车四下环顾时并不觉得开心。他这次南下不得不乘坐黑人专列，为此，他就已经感到很恼火了。如今，这座又脏又乱的小镇，镇里这些又黑又脏的面孔都使他闷闷不乐。他对这些高高兴兴前来迎接他的人群无话可说。人们也很快就对他感到纳闷。这个冷冰冰的、沉默寡言的人是他们的约翰吗？他们盼望他的归来盼了那么久，总算把他盼回来了，可是却根本见不到他的笑脸，听不见他的笑声，更没有他那友好的握手问候，这一切都跑到哪儿去了呢？

---

excited *adj.* 激动的；兴奋的
unhappy *adj.* 不快乐的
dirty *adj.* 肮脏的
handshake *n.* 握手

"He seems rather serious," said the *minister* of the church. "Or too proud for us?" his neighbor wondered. But the white mailman, passing by, said, "That fool black boy went north and got full of *foolish* ideas. But they won't work in Altamaha." The other whites agreed.

The welcome—home party at the church that night was a failure. Rain spoiled the *barbeque*. The ice cream *melted*. John was still cold and silent, and people didn't understand what was wrong. Then it was time for John to speak. He told his people that the world was changing. He spoke about the need for blacks to work to change the color line. More schools were needed, and better jobs. Blacks needed to forget their differences. They needed to work together to

---

"他好像挺严肃，"教堂的牧师说。他的邻居也很纳闷，说，"也许是对我们太傲慢了？"但那白人邮差打这儿经过时却说："那个傻孩子去北方灌回来满脑子傻念头。可是，那些东西在阿尔塔玛哈可行不通。"其他白人也都表示赞同。

当晚在教堂举行的接风晚宴很不成功。露天烤肉因下雨而泡汤，冰淇淋也融化了。约翰还是那样冷漠无言，大家都闹不明白这到底是怎么回事。该约翰讲话了。他告诉乡亲们：这个世界正在变革。他谈到黑人要行动起来消除种族界线，要建立更多的学校，要有较好的工作，还要忘掉自身的差异。黑人要共同努力来改善生活。

---

minister *n.* 牧师
barbeque *n.* 烤肉野餐
foolish *adj.* 愚蠢的
melt *v.* 融化

make better lives.

When he finished, the church was silent. People looked at *each other* in surprise. They didn't understand John. He had changed. He was not the boy they had known. He had become different from them.

John walked quietly out of the church. He stood alone in the *darkness*. His sister Jennie followed him.

"John," she said softly, "does it make everyone unhappy when they study and learn lots of things?"

He smiled at her. "I'm afraid it does," he said.

"And John, are you glad you studied?"

"Yes," he answered slowly. But he *sounded* sure of himself.

他讲完后，教堂里鸦雀无声。惊讶之余，人们你看看我，我看看你，都不明白约翰说了些什么。他们只是觉得他变了，不再是他们所熟悉的约翰了。他已经变得与众不同了。

约翰平静地走出教堂，独自站在夜色中。小妹珍妮跟在他后边。

"约翰，"她温柔地说，"是不是人念了书，学到很多东西，就会觉得不开心？"

约翰对她笑了笑，说："恐怕是这样。"

"那么，约翰，你很高兴自己念过书吗？"

"高兴，"他说得很慢，但听起来很自信。

---

each other 彼此；互相

darkness *n.* 黑暗

sound *v.* 听起来

Jennie said thoughtfully, "I wish I was unhappy, John. And—and—I think I am a little unhappy." She put her arms around him.

A few days later, John went up to the Judge's house. He wanted to ask if he could become the teacher at the school for black children.

The Judge met him at the front door. "Go around to the back door and wait, John," he said. His face was unfriendly.

John sat on the ***kitchen*** stairs and waited. "I keep making mistakes," he said to himself. "Everything I do is wrong. I came home to help my people. But even before I left the train ***station***, I hurt their feelings. I wanted to teach them what I think about the color line, and they don't understand. I told myself to show respect to the

---

珍妮若有所思地说："我倒希望自己不开心，约翰。而且——而且——我觉得我也确实有点不开心。"说着，她伸出双臂搂住了哥哥。

几天后，约翰去法官家拜访，想问问他能否在黑人学校当老师。

法官到前门见了他。"绕到后门去等着，约翰，"他说。他的表情很不友好。

约翰坐在后厨的台阶上等着。"我一再出错，"他对自己说。"我不管做什么都不对。我回到家乡是要帮助我们的人，可没出车站就伤了他们的

---

kitchen *n.* 厨房　　station *n.* 车站

Judge. But then I go to his front door. I should know better!"

Just then Jennie opened the kitchen door. She said the Judge would see him now. When he went in, the Judge didn't ask him to sit down. Right away, he said,"You want to teach school, I suppose. Well, John, I want to tell you something. You know I am a friend of your people. I've helped your family. I would have helped you more if you hadn't gone away North. Now, I like you colored people. But you and I both know that in this country black people can't be equal to whites. You can be good and ***respectful*** workers. And I will try to help you. But the question is—will you teach your people to be good workers, like their mothers and fathers are? I knew your father, John. He ***belonged to*** my brother. He was a good black. Will you be like

---

心；我想告诉他们自己对种族界线的看法，而他们又不理解；我告诫自己要尊敬法官，却又去走他的前门。我本该知道这些呀！”

这时，珍妮打开了厨房的门，说法官要见他。他进了屋，那法官并没有让他坐下，开口就说：“我想你是要教书。那么，约翰，我得告诉你一些事儿。你知道我是你们黑人的朋友，我帮助过你们家。假如你没去北方的话，我还会给你们更多的帮助。可见，我喜欢你们黑人，但你我都知道，在这个国家里，黑人不可能与白人平等。你们可以做守规矩懂礼貌的劳动者，我也会尽力帮助你们。可问题是——你会教你们的人去好好干活吗？就像他们的父母那样？我认识你父亲，约翰，他是我兄弟的奴隶，是个本分的黑人。你

---

respectful *adj.* 恭敬的

belong to 属于

him? Or will you try to put foolish ideas in people's heads? Will you spoil them by making them think they are equal to whites?"

"I know how things are here," John quickly answered. But the Judge looked at him, and wondered.

V

A month after John opened the school for black children, the Judge's son came home. This other John was tall and blond and sure of himself. His family was so proud of him. The whole white town was glad to see him come home. But things did not ***go well*** between John and his father. The Judge wanted his son to stay in Altamaha. He hoped his son would be a leader in town, like himself. But John thought the town was small and uninteresting—very boring, ***in fact***. "Nothing here but dirt and blacks," he would say. "What could

---

会和他一样吗？还是会一个劲儿地把一些愚蠢的想法灌输到别人的脑袋里？你会让他们认为自己和白人是平等的，从而毁了他们吗？"

"我知道这里是什么情况，"约翰赶忙回答。然而法官还是疑惑地看着他。

V

约翰给黑人孩子们上了一个月的课后，法官的儿子回来了。这个约翰个头很高，金发碧眼，充满自信。全家人都为他感到自豪。全城的白人都为他的归来而高兴。可是约翰和他父亲的相处并不愉快。这位法官想让儿子留在阿尔塔玛哈，和自己一样，当镇上的长官。而约翰认为这个城镇太小，没意思——说白了，是非常无聊。"这里除了灰尘和黑鬼以外什么都没有，"他

---

go well　进展顺利

in fact　事实上；实际上

be more boring than that?" And he and the Judge would *argue* about it.

One evening when they were arguing about John's *future*, the mailman came to visit.

"I hear John's getting everybody excited over at the black school," he said.

"What do you mean?" asked the Judge.

"Oh, nothing much. Just, he talks to them about respect, and *equality*. About not saying 'sir' to a white man. Things like that."

"Who is this John?" asked the Judge's son.

"Why, it's little black John. You *used to* play with him," answered the Judge.

总是这么说。"有什么比这更无聊呢？"他和法官于是就争辩起来。

一天傍晚，他们还在就约翰的前途问题争论不休时，那个邮差登门来访。

"我听说约翰在黑人学校里把大伙儿的情绪都给煽动起来了，"他说。

"你是什么意思？"法官问。

"哦，也没什么。就是，他对他们讲什么尊重啊，平等啊，对白人不用称呼'先生'啊，等等，诸如此类的事情。"

"这个约翰是谁？"法官的儿子问。

"怎么，不记得了？就是小黑约翰。以前你还和他玩呢，"法官回答说。

---

argue *v.* 争论；辩论
equality *n.* 平等
future *n.* 未来；前途
used to 过去常常

John looked angry, but then he laughed. "Oh," he said, "I saw him in New York. That's the black man that tried to ***push*** in and sit next to the lady I was with..."

But the Judge had heard enough. All day, he had been feeling angry with his own John. Now it was time to do something about the other John. He went right to the school house door.

"John!" the Judge called out. His face was red with anger. "This school is closed. You children, go home and get to work. The white people of Altamaha are not spending their money on colored people just to fill their heads with foolish ideas! Go home! I'll close the door myself!"

Back at the Judge's house, his son ***looked around*** for something to do. He was ***bored*** with everything. His father's books were old, the

---

约翰顿时面有愠色，但却笑了起来。“哈，”他说，“我在纽约见过他。就是那个拼命往人群里挤的黑人，还坐到了和我在一起的女士身边……”

法官早已听得不耐烦，一整天，他都在跟自己的约翰生气，现在，该收拾收拾另一个约翰了。于是，他便直奔学校大门而去。

“约翰！”法官吼叫着，满脸气得通红。“这所学校关闭。你们这帮小子，都回家干活去。阿尔塔玛哈的白人不能往黑人身上花这个冤枉钱，让他们往脑子里灌愚蠢的想法！回家去！我要亲自关闭校门！”

再回到法官家里。他的儿子正百无聊赖，四处打量，不知能干点什么。

---

push *v.* 推进；推

look around 环顾四周

bored *adj.* 无聊的；无趣的

town newspaper was foolish. He tried to sleep, but it was too hot. Finally, he walked out into the fields. "I feel like I'm in prison," he thought to himself. John wasn't really a bad young man. Just a little spoiled. And he was so sure of himself, like his proud father. "There isn't even a pretty girl around here," he said angrily.

Just then, he saw Jennie coming down the road. "I never noticed what a pretty girl she is!" he said to himself. "Hello, Jennie," he called out to her. "You haven't even given me a ***kiss*** since I came home!"

Jennie looked at him with surprise. She smiled respectfully and tried to ***pass by***. But John was bored, and felt like playing with her. He took her arm. She was afraid, and turned and ***ran away***. John ran after her.

父亲的书过时了，镇里的报纸又很荒唐。想睡觉，天又太热。最后，他出了门，来到田里。"真像蹲监狱，"他心里想。约翰并不真是坏青年，他只是有点被宠坏了。像他高傲的父亲一样，他也很自信。"周围连个漂亮姑娘都没有，"他生气地说。

就在这时，他看见珍妮沿马路走来。"我以前怎么没注意到她长得这么漂亮！"他自言自语说。"你好，珍妮，"他对她大声说。"我回来后你还没吻过我呢！"

珍妮吃惊地看着他，恭敬地一笑，就想走过去。可是约翰觉得很无聊，就想跟她取乐。他抓住她的胳膊，她吓得转身就跑，约翰就在后面追。

---

kiss *n.* 吻　　pass by 经过；走过

run away 逃跑

Jennie's brother John was coming down the road. His heart was sad, and his thoughts were angry. "I can't live here anymore," he was thinking. "I'll go north and find work. I'll bring Mother and Jennie with me." He had never been so unhappy.

Suddenly he saw his sister in front of him. He heard her cry out in fear. John could see she was trying to ***escape*** from the arms of the tall, blond man. Without thinking, John picked up a tree branch. He hit the Judge's son hard, on the head. The young man fell down. His face was ***covered*** with ***blood***.

John walked slowly home. "Mammy, I'm going away," he said. "I'm going to be free."

"Are you going North, son? Are you going North again?"

"Yes, Mammy, I'm going... North."

珍妮的哥哥约翰正朝这边走来。他很伤心，也很气愤。“我在这儿再也待不下去了，”他想。“我要去北方找工作，带着妈妈和珍妮。”他以前从来没有这样沮丧过。

突然，他看见自己的妹妹在前面，也听到了她的惊叫。他看出她正在奋力挣脱一个高个子金发男子的臂膀。约翰不假思索地拣起一根树枝，使劲地抽打法官的儿子，抽打他的脑袋。那小子倒下了，满脸是血。

约翰慢慢地走回家。“妈妈，我要走了，”他说。“我就要自由了。”

“你要去北方吗，儿子？你还要去北方吗？”

“是的，妈妈，我要去……北方。”

---

escape *v.* 逃避；逃跑

covered *adj.* 覆盖着的

blood *n.* 血；血液

John walked slowly back down the road to wait for the white men. He saw blood on the ground where John's white body had ***fallen***. They had played together as boys. He wondered where those little boys had gone. He thought about his life in the North. He seemed to hear again the singing from the beautiful music hall. Listen! But maybe it was only the men coming to get him. As he waited and listened, the sound became louder and louder, like a storm coming. He saw the old Judge, leading the other men. His face was white, his eyes red with anger. John felt sorry for him—so sorry. Then the men ***reached*** him, and the storm broke all around him.

And the world ***whistled*** in his ears.

约翰沿着刚才的路慢慢地走了回去，他要等着白人来找他算账。他看到在约翰白色身体倒下的地方有血迹。小时候他们一起玩过。他不知道那两个小男孩如今都去了哪里。他想起自己在北方的生活，他好像又听到了从美丽的音乐厅里传来的歌声。听！但那也可能是那些人要来抓他了。他一边等一边听，声音越来越大，像暴风雨即将来临。他看见了老法官，领着一帮人。他的脸气得煞白，眼睛气得通红。约翰觉得对不起他——很对不起。一转眼，那些人都上来了，一场疾风暴雨扑面而来。

于是，世界就在他耳边鸣响。

---

fall *v.* 摔倒；跌倒　　reach *v.* 到达；抵达

whistle *v.* 吹口哨；鸣汽笛

The Lady, or the Tiger?

Adapted from the story by Frank R. Stockton

Frank R. Stockton was born in 1834. His most famous stories are in the form of fairy tales, ghost stories, or romances. But in all of them his humor has an edge like a knife. When"The Lady, or the Tiger?" appeared in *Century Magazine* in 1882, it caused ***excitement*** all over the country. Hundreds of people wrote letters to the magazine or to their newspapers about it. Many letters demanded an answer to the question that the story asks. Others asked if the story was really about government, or ***psychology***, or

是美女，还是老虎?

根据弗兰克·R. 斯托克顿的同名故事改编

弗兰克·R. 斯托克顿生于1834年。他最擅长写作神话故事、鬼怪故事和爱情故事。但不管是哪一类故事，都含有犀利的幽默。1882年“是美女，还是老虎?”首次发表在《世纪杂志》上，激起了全国上下众多读者的极大兴趣。成百上千的人为此给杂志社或当地报纸写信。其中很多人都要求对故事中提出的问题给出答案，还有人问该故事是否与政府、心理学、两性间的矛盾或其他问题有关。斯托克顿很明智，他

excitement *n.* 兴奋；激动

psychology *n.* 心理学

The Lady, or the Tiger?

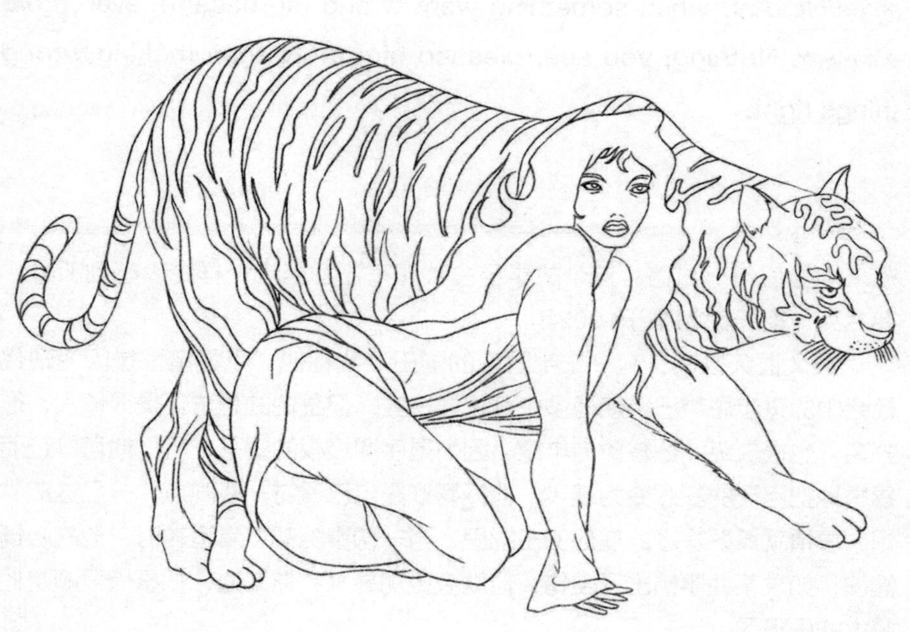

the battle of the sexes, or something else. Wisely, Stockton never answered any of the letters. The story remains as fresh today as it was then. Frank Stockton died in 1902.

A long, long time ago, there was a semi-barbaric king. I call him semi-barbaric because the modern world, with its modern ideas, had softened his ***barbarism*** a little. But still, his ideas were large, wild, and free. He had a wonderful ***imagination***. He was also a king of the greatest powers, and he easily turned the dreams of his imagination into facts. He greatly enjoyed talking to himself about ideas. And, when he and himself agreed upon a thing, the thing was done. He was a very pleasant man when everything in his world moved ***smoothly***. And when something went wrong, he became even more ***pleasant***. Nothing, you see, pleased him more than making wrong things right.

从未回复任何一封信。这个故事至今读起来还和当年一样令人感到新鲜。弗兰克·斯托克顿卒于1902年。

很久很久以前，有一个半野蛮的国王。我称他“半野蛮”是因为现代社会中的进步思想已经使他多少开化了一些。但是他的想法还是很惊人，很野蛮，也很放纵。他想象力丰富。因为是手握极权的国王，所以他可以轻而易举地把自己的梦想变为现实。他很喜欢跟自己探讨一些观点，一旦达成共识，事情就算解决了。在他的王国里，当一切事务都正常运转时，他就心情愉快；如果某些事情出了差错，他就会更加高兴。你知道，把事情理顺是他最大的乐事了。

---

barbarism *n.* 野蛮行为

imagination *n.* 想象力

smoothly *adv.* 流畅地；流利地

pleasant *adj.* 令人愉快的

One of this semi-barbaric king's modern ideas was the idea of a large ***arena***. In this arena, his people could watch both men and animals in acts of ***bravery***.

But even this modern idea was touched by the king's wild imagination. In his arena, the people saw more than soldiers fighting soldiers, or men fighting animals. They enjoyed more than the sight of blood. In the king's arena, the people saw the laws of the country at work. They saw good men lifted up and bad men pushed down. Most important, they were able to watch the workings of the First Law of Chance.

Here is what happened when a man was accused of a ***crime***. If the king was interested in the crime, then the people were told to come to the arena. They came together and sat there, thousands of them. The king sat high up in his king's chair. When he gave a sign,

---

这个半野蛮国王有个时髦的想法，那就是开个大竞技场。在场内，他的臣民能观赏到人与动物之间的生死较量。

可就连这个时髦想法也受到了他那野蛮思想的殃及。在他的竞技场里，人们看到的不仅仅是士兵之间的交战，或人兽之间的较量。尽览血战之余，他们还能亲眼看见国家法律的实施。他们看到好人洗冤释放，坏人遭受惩罚。更重要的是，他们能够观望“碰大运法”的整个实施过程。

当一个人被起诉有罪时，就会出现下面的情况：如果国王对此案感兴趣，就会通知民众到竞技场来。成千上万的人进来坐下，国王高高地坐在王位上。他打个手势，他座位下面的门就会打开。被告通过这个门走进竞技

---

arena *n.* 竞技场

bravery *n.* 勇敢；勇气

crime *n.* 罪；犯罪

a door below him opened. The accused man stepped out into the arena. Across from him, on the other side of the arena, were two other doors. They were close together and they looked the same. The accused man would walk straight to these doors and open one of them. He could choose either one of the doors. He was ***forced*** by nothing and led by no one. Only Chance helped him—or didn't help him.

Behind one of the doors was a tiger. It was the wildest, biggest, hungriest tiger that could be found. Of course, it quickly jumped on the man. The man quickly—or not so quickly—died. After he died, sad ***bells*** rang, women cried, and the thousands of people walked home slowly.

But, if the ***accused*** man opened the other door, a lady would step out. She was the finest and most ***beautiful*** lady that could be found.

场。在他对面，也就是竞技场的另一侧，还有两扇门。这两扇门挨在一起，看上去一模一样。被告径直走过去，打开一扇。他可以在两扇中任选一扇，没有任何人强迫，也没有任何人引导，天助与否——全凭"运气"。

其中一个门里藏着老虎，那是所能找到的最具野性、个头最大、饥饿感最强的老虎。当然，它会飞快地跃到那人身上，他也会很快地——或者不那么快地——死掉。他死后，丧钟鸣起，妇女号哭，成千上万的人慢慢地走回家去。

但是，如果被告开的是另一扇门，一位女士就会走出来。她是当今最贤淑、最美丽的女子。就在当时当地，她就得嫁给被告。不管这个男人是否

---

force *v.* 强迫；迫使
accused *adj.* 被控告的
bell *n.* 铃；钟
beautiful *adj.* 美丽的

At that moment, there in the arena, she would be married to the man. It didn't matter if the man was already married. It didn't matter if he was in love with another woman. The king did not let little things like that get in the way of his imagination. No, the two were married there in front of the king. There was music and dancing. Then happy bells rang, women cried, and the thousands of people walked home singing.

This was the way the law worked in the king's semi-barbaric country. Its *fairness* is clear. The *criminal* could not know which door the lady was behind. He opened either door as he wanted. At the moment he opened the door, he did not know if he was going to be eaten or married.

The people of the country thought the law was a good one. They went to the arena with great interest. They never knew if they would see a bloody killing or a lovely *marriage*. This *uncertainty* gave the day

---

已婚，也不管他是否正爱着别的女人。国王决不会让这些琐事妨碍自己的想象，决不，这两个人要在国王面前就地成婚。场上音乐奏起，载歌载舞。欢乐的钟声响起，妇女喜极而泣，成千上万的观众唱着歌儿走回家去。

在国王半野蛮的国家中，这条法律就是这样实施的。它的公平之处显而易见：罪犯不可能知道哪个门里藏着美女。他想开哪个门就开哪个门。开门的那一刻，他不知道自己是要被吃掉，还是要结婚。

这个国家的臣民都认为这是一条公平的法律。他们兴致勃勃地去竞技场，从不知道自己即将看的究竟是血腥的杀戮，还是浪漫的婚礼。这一不确定性赋予那个日子以美妙的、不同寻常的感觉。他们喜欢的是这条法律的公

---

fairness *n.* 公平；公正
criminal *n.* 罪犯
marriage *n.* 婚姻
uncertainty *n.* 不确定

its fine and unusual taste. And they liked the fairness of the law. Wasn't it true that the accused man held his life in his own hands?

This semi-barbaric king had a daughter. The princess was as beautiful as any flower in the king's imagination. She had a mind as wild and free as the king's. She had a heart like a *volcano*. The king loved her deeply, watched her closely, and was very *jealous* of her. But he could not always watch her. And in his *castle* lived a young man. This young man was a worker. He was a good worker, but he was of low birth. He was brave and *handsome*, and the princess loved him, and was jealous of him. Because of the girl's semi-barbarism, her love was hot and strong. Of course, the young man quickly returned it. The lovers were happy together for many months. But one day the king discovered their love. Of course he did not lose a minute. He threw the young man into prison and named a day for his appearance in the arena.

正性。被告手中掌握着自己的命运，难道这不是千真万确的吗？

这个半野蛮国王有个女儿。公主在国王的想象中美若鲜花。她的头脑和国王的一样野蛮而又放纵，她的心像一座火山。国王深深地爱着她，密切地关注着她，也非常忧心和警惕地看着她。可他又不可能寸步不离地看着她。在他的城堡里有个年轻人，是个劳工，而且是一把好手，但出身卑微。他性格勇敢，相貌英俊。公主爱他，也猜忌他。公主的半野蛮使她对年轻人的爱火热而强烈。当然，年轻人也很快爱上了她。这对恋人甜甜蜜蜜地过了几个月。但是，有一天国王发现了他们之间的爱情，于是，当机立断，把年轻人投入监狱，然后，定下一个日子让他在竞技场上出现。

---

volcano *n.* 火山
castle *n.* 城堡
jealous *adj.* 妒忌的；猜疑的
handsome *adj.* 英俊的

There had never been a day as important as that one. The country was searched for the strongest, biggest, most dangerous tiger. With equal care, the country was searched for the finest and most beautiful young woman. There was no question, of course, that the young man had loved the princess. He knew it, she knew it, the king knew it, and everybody else knew it, too. But the king did not let this stand in the way of his *excellent* law. Also, the king knew that the young man would now *disappear* from his daughter's life. He would disappear with the other beautiful lady. Or he would disappear into the hungry tiger. The only question was, "Which?"

And so the day arrived. Thousands and thousands of people came to the arena. The king was in his place, *across from* those two doors that seemed alike but were *truly* very different.

这是有史以来从未有过的重要日子。全国上下都在搜寻最强壮、最高大、最凶猛的老虎，也以同样的慎重搜寻最贤淑、最漂亮的年轻女子。毫无疑问，那个年轻人爱着公主。他知道，公主知道，国王知道，其他人也都知道。但是国王决不让这件事妨碍他那卓群的法律的实施。而且，国王明白，这个年轻人会从他女儿的生活中消失，要么和另一个漂亮的女子一起消失，要么消失在那只饿虎的肚子里。唯一的问题是，到底是“哪一种？”

这一天如期而至。数以万计的人来到竞技场。国王坐在自己的位置上，对面是那两扇看似相同，实则迥异的门。

---

excellent *adj.* 卓越的
disappear *v.* 消失
across from 在……对面
truly *adv.* 真实地

All was ready. The sign was given. The door below the king opened, and the lover of the princess walked into the arena. Tall, handsome, fair, he seemed like a ***prince***. The people had not known that such a fine young man had lived among them. Was it any wonder that the princess had loved him?

The young man came forward into the arena, and then turned toward the king's chair. But his eyes were not on the king. They were on the princess, who sat to her father's right. Perhaps it was wrong for the young lady to be there. But remember that she was still semi-barbaric. Her wild heart would not let her be away from her ***lover*** on this day. More important, she now knew the secret of the doors. Over the past few days, she had used all of her power in the castle, and much of her gold. She had ***discovered*** which door hid the tiger,

---

一切准备就绪。手势已经打出。国王座位下面的门开了，公主的心上人走进了竞技场。他身材魁伟，相貌英俊，肤色白皙，满头金发，俨然一位王子。人们以前从不知晓在他们当中居然还有如此出众的男人，难怪公主会爱上他！

年轻人举步进入竞技场，把头转向国王的座椅。可是他的目光并不在国王身上，而是在公主身上——她就坐在父亲的右边。年轻的公主也许不该在这里出现。但是，别忘了，她可还是半野蛮的。她那颗野蛮的心不会让她在这一天离开她的心上人。更重要的是，她现在握有两扇门的秘密。在过去的几天里，她动用了自己在城堡中的所有权力，也花了不少金钱，终于得知哪

---

prince *n.* 王子
lover *n.* 爱人；恋人
discover *v.* 发现

and which door hid the lady.

She knew more than this. She knew the lady. It was one of the fairest and loveliest ladies in the castle. In fact, this lady was more than fair and lovely. She was *thoughtful*, kind, loving, full of laughter, and quick of mind. The princess hated her. She had seen, or imagined she had seen, the lady looking at the young man. She thought these looks had been noticed and even returned. Once or twice she had seen them talking together. Perhaps they had talked for only a moment. Perhaps they had *talked of* nothing important. But how could the princess *be sure of* that? The other girl was lovely and kind, yes. But she had lifted her eyes to the lover of the princess. And so, in her semi-barbaric heart, the princess was jealous, and *hated* her.

扇门后藏着老虎，哪个门后藏着美女。

此外，她还认识那个美女。那是城堡中最美丽、最可爱的女子之一。其实，那个女子不仅美丽、可爱，她还很有头脑，为人善良，富有爱心，性格开朗，思维敏捷。公主恨她。公主曾看见过，或在想象中看见过，这个女子注视着那个年轻人。她觉得那个年轻人注意到了这一点，而且也注视着那个女子。有一两次，她还看到他们两人在一起说话，也许仅说了片刻，也许只说些无关紧要的事。可公主怎么能肯定呢？那个女孩的确又可爱，又善良。可她竟敢抬眼去看公主的心上人。于是，在公主那半野蛮的心里便埋下了忌恨的种子。

---

thoughtful *adj.* 深思的；体贴的

be sure of 确信；确定

talk of 谈到；谈及

hate *v.* 憎恨

Now, in the arena, her lover turned and looked at her. His eyes met hers, and he saw ***at once*** that she knew the secret of the doors. He had been sure that she would know it. He understood her heart. He had known that she would try to learn this thing which no one else knew—not even the king. He had known she would try. And now, as he looked at her, he saw that she had succeeded.

At that moment, his quick and worried look asked the question: "Which?" This question in his eyes was as clear to the princess as spoken words. There was no time to lose. The question had been asked in a second. It must be answered in a second.

Her right arm ***rested*** on the arm of her chair. She ***lifted*** her hand and made a quick ***movement*** towards the right. No one saw except her lover. Every eye except his was on the man in the arena.

如今，在竞技场上，她的爱人转过身来看着她。四目相对，他立即看出她知道那两扇门的秘密。他一直相信她会知道的。他了解她的心。他知道她会尽力去获取这个其他任何人，包括国王在内，都不知道的信息。他早就知道她会竭尽全力。现在，他看着她，心里明白她已经稳操胜券了。

此时，他用焦虑的眼神在问："哪一个？"他眼神里的这个问题对公主来说是不言而喻的。时间紧迫，一刻也不能耽搁。问题在瞬间提出，也必须在瞬间回答。

她的右臂放在椅子的扶手上，她抬起手迅速地向右边动了一下。这个动作，除了她的爱人以外没人看见，因为除了他以外，所有的人都把目光集中在场上，集中在他的身上。

---

at once 立刻；马上

rest *v.* 靠某物支撑

lift *v.* 举起

movement *n.* 动作；姿势

He turned and walked quickly across the *empty* space. Every heart stopped beating. Every breath was held. Every eye was fixed upon that man. Without stopping for even a second, he went to the door on the right and opened it.

Now, the question is this: Did the tiger come out of that door, or did the lady?

As we think deeply about this question, it becomes harder and harder to answer. We must know the heart of the animal called man. And the heart is difficult to know. Think of it, dear reader, and remember that the decision is not yours. The *decision* belongs to that hot-blooded, semi-barbaric princess. Her heart was at a white heat beneath the fires of jealousy and *painful* sadness. She had lost him, but who should have him?

他转身快步穿过场地。在场的每一颗心都停止了跳动，每一个人都屏住了呼吸，每一双眼睛都盯着那个人。他毫不犹豫地走向右边，把门打开了。

现在的问题是，门里出来的是老虎呢，还是美女?

对这个问题，我们越是陷入沉思，就越发觉得难以回答。我们必须了解那被称作“人”的动物的心，而人心是难以捉摸的。想想吧，亲爱的读者，要记住，那决定不是你做出的，而是那个热血沸腾的、半野蛮的公主做出的。她的心在燃烧的炉火和痛苦的悲伤中已经白热化。她失去了他，可谁又该拥有他呢?

---

empty *adj.* 空的

decision *n.* 决定；决心

painful *adj.* 痛苦的

Very often, in her thoughts and in her dreams, she had cried out in fear. She had imagined her lover as he opened the door to the hungry tiger.

And even more often she had seen him at the other door! She had bitten her *tongue* and pulled her hair. She had hated his happiness when he opened the door to the lady. Her heart burned with pain and *hatred* when she imagined the *scene*: He goes quickly to meet the woman. He leads her into the arena. His eyes shine with new life. The happy bells ring wildly. The two of them are married before her eyes. Children run around them and throw flowers. There is music, and the thousands of people dance in the streets. And the princess's cry of *sadness* is lost in the sounds of happiness!

Wouldn't it be better for him to die at once? Couldn't he wait for

---

有很多次，在沉思默想中，在睡梦中，她都惊恐地大声喊叫。她想象着自己的爱人打开了那扇通向饿虎的大门。

有更多次，她看到他去开另一扇门。她又是咬舌头，又是扯头发。她不愿意看到他打开通向美女之门后所获得的幸福。一想到那个场景，她的心就在痛苦与怨恨中燃烧：他疾步上前去见那个女人，把她领到竞技场，目光中闪耀着新生的喜悦。幸福的钟声疯狂地敲响。两个人就在她痛苦的注视下成婚。孩子们围着他们又跑又跳，往他们身上抛撒鲜花。伴着音乐，成千上万的人在大街上载歌载舞。公主悲伤的哭声被淹没在欢声笑语中。

他若能马上死去岂不更好？难道他不能在那个美丽的半野蛮的未来世界

---

tongue *n.* 舌头

hatred *n.* 憎恨；怨恨

scene *n.* 场面；场景

sadness *n.* 悲哀

her in the beautiful land of the semi-barbaric future?

But the tiger, those cries of pain, that ***blood***!

Her decision had been shown in a second. But it had been made after days and nights of deep and painful thought. She had known she would be asked. She had decided what to answer. She had moved her hand to the right.

The question of her decision is not an easy one to think about. Certainly I am not the one person who should have to answer it. So I leave it with all of you: Which came out of the opened door—the lady, or the tiger?

里等候她吗?

可是，那老虎，那痛苦的悲号，那鲜血啊！

她的决定是在瞬间亮相的，然而，做出这个决定却是经过了无数个日日夜夜沉痛的思考！她知道他会向她询问，她也决定了应该怎样回答。她把手移向右侧。

她作了什么样的决定，这个问题实在难以琢磨。当然，这个问题也并非应该由我来回答。所以，我把问题留给你们大家：门开了，走出来的究竟是哪一个？——是美女，还是老虎?

---

blood *n.* 血；血液

How I Went to the Mines

Adapted from the story by Bret Harte

Bret Harte was born in Albany, New York, in 1836. His father was a schoolteacher who died young. His mother *remarried* and moved to San Francisco. When Harte was seventeen, he moved there to join his mother and her second husband. In California, Harte turned to *journalism* and short story writing after trying several other jobs. For a while he was an unsuccessful gold *miner*. His story "How I Went to the Mines" came from that experience. In 1868, he became

淘金记

根据布赖特·哈特的同名故事改写

布赖特·哈特1836年生于纽约州的奥尔巴尼。父亲是一位小学教师，英年早逝，母亲改嫁到旧金山。哈特17岁时去跟母亲和继父同住。在加州，在尝试过几个工作之后转而从事新闻工作和写作。有一段时间，他淘金喜获成功。故事“淘金记”就是取材于那次经历。1868

remarry *v.* 再婚　　journalism *n.* 新闻业
miner *n.* 矿工

the first editor of the magazine *Overland Monthly*. In the same year he published a story, "The Luck of Roaring Camp," that brought him national fame. Harte is generally considered to be the first American writer of stories of "local color"—that is, stories about a special place, its people, and its way of life. When his stories about the West made him famous, he went East to write for the *Atlantic Monthly* for $10,000 a year (a very large amount in those days). But neither this success nor his ***popularity*** as a writer lasted long. As a result, he left the United States in 1877 to work as a businessman and U.S. ***consul*** in Europe. He finally ***settled*** in England in 1885, where he lived and continued to publish books until his death in 1902.

I

I had been in ***California*** for two years before I thought of going

---

年，他成为《大陆月刊》杂志第一任编辑，同年发表了故事“咆哮营的幸运儿”，使他在国内一举成名。他被公认为是第一位描写带有“乡土色彩”的故事的美国短篇小说作家——也就是描写某个特殊的地方和那里的人们及其生活方式。当这些描写西部的故事使他成名后，他又到东部为《大西洋月刊》杂志撰稿，年薪10,000美元（在当时是一笔巨款）。但他的成功和作为一个作家的声望并没有持久。后来，哈特于1877年离开美国前往欧洲，做过生意，也当过美国驻欧领事。1885年定居英国后，便一直生活在那里并继续发表作品，直到1902年逝世。

I

我想去淘金之前已经在加州生活了两年。开始淘金多少有些迫不得已。

---

popularity *n.* 普及；流行
consul *n.* 领事
settle *v.* 定居
california *n.* 加利福尼亚

to the mines. My introduction to gold digging was partly forced on me. I was the somewhat youthful and, I fear, not very experienced schoolmaster of a small pioneer ***settlement***. Our school was only partly paid for by the state; most of the cost was carried by a few families in the settlement. When two families—and about a dozen children—moved away to a richer and newer district, the school was ***immediately*** closed.

In twenty-four hours, I was without both students and ***employment***. I am afraid I missed the children the most: I had made ***companions*** and friends of some of them. I stood that bright May morning before an empty schoolhouse in the wild woods. I felt strange to think that our little summer "play" at being schoolmaster and student was over. I remember clearly a parting gift from a student a year older than I.

我本是一个多少有些年轻稚嫩，恐怕还有点经验不足的小学教师。这是一个早期移民小社区的小学，只享有一部分州政府拨款，办学经费多数得由社区里的一些住户自筹。当其中的两户——他们有十几个孩子——迁到较为富裕的新开发地区时，学校即刻停办了。

二十四小时后，我就成了光杆司令，既无学生也无工作。恐怕我最思念的是学生，因为我跟其中一些已经成了同伴和朋友。一个晴朗的五月上午，我站在原始森林前空荡荡的校舍，想到在夏天里扮演教师和学生的小“游戏”已经结束，心里不禁有些异样的感觉。我清楚地记得一个比我还大一岁的学生送给我的离别纪念物。那是一大块姜饼。它在旅途中可真帮了我大

---

settlement *n.* 移民；殖民
immediately *adv.* 立即；立刻
employment *n.* 职业；雇佣
companion *n.* 同伴；朋友

He gave me a huge piece of ***gingerbread***. It helped me greatly in my journeys, for I was alone in the world at that moment, and by nature ***extravagant*** with money.

I had been frightfully extravagant even on my small schoolmaster's pay. I had spent much money on fine shirts. I gave as an excuse that I should set an example in dress for my students. The result, however, was that at this important moment, I had only seven dollars in my pocket. I spent five on a second-hand ***revolver*** that I felt was necessary to show that I was leaving peaceful employment for one of risk and adventure.

For I had finally decided to go to the mines and become a gold digger. Other employment, and my few friends in San Francisco, were expensively distant. The nearest mining district was only forty

---

忙，因为我当时完全是孤身一人，而且天生喜欢挥霍金钱。

就连那微薄的教师工薪我也无度地挥霍。我花好多钱买质地优良的衬衫，借口我得在衣着打扮上给学生树立榜样。然而，结果怎样？在这个重要时刻，口袋里只剩下区区七美元。我花五美元买了一把二手的左轮手枪，我觉得有必要表明我离开安宁的职业是为了寻求冒险和刺激。

最终我决定去金矿当一个淘金者。要想干其他职业，或去投靠旧金山仅有的几个朋友，对我来说，都显得路途遥远，财力不足。最近的矿区只有

---

gingerbread *n.* 姜饼

extravagant *adj.* 奢侈的；挥霍的

revolver *n.* 左轮手枪

miles away. My hope was that when I got there I would find a miner named Jim I had met once in San Francisco. With only his name to help me, I expected to find him somewhere in the mines. But my remaining two dollars was not enough for travel by horse and ***wagon***. I must walk to the mines, and I did.

I cannot clearly remember how I did it. The end of the first day found me with painfully ***blistered*** feet. I realized that the shiny leather shoes, so proper for a schoolmaster, were not suited to my wanderings. But I held on to them as a sign of my past life. I carried them in my hands when pain and pride caused me to leave the highway and travel barefoot on the ***trails***.

I'm afraid all my belongings looked ***unsuitable***. The few travelers I met on the road looked at me and tried not to smile. I had a fine old

---

四十英里远。我怀着一种希望，想去那儿找一个名叫吉姆的矿工，这人我以前在旧金山见过。我只知道他的名字，仅凭这个，我就想去那个矿区找他。但我剩下的两美元根本不够骑马和坐车，我必须徒步到矿区去，于是就徒步去了。

我记不太清自己究竟是怎么走去的。第一天结束时，我双脚全都起了水泡，疼痛难忍。我意识到那双光亮的皮鞋在当小学教师的时候倒是蛮合适，但对于目前这种流浪来说可就不适宜了。但我仍然坚持穿皮鞋，以此标明我过去的生活。实在疼痛难忍时，我就离开了公路走小路，以便把鞋脱下来用手提着，然后光着脚走。怎么说我也得保留一份自尊哪。

我总担心随身携带的物品看起来不匹配。在路上碰到的少数几个行人看着我时都强忍着笑。我有一个质地上乘的老式皮包，那是我母亲给我的，还

---

wagon *n.* 四轮马车
blister *v.* 起水泡
trail *n.* 小径；小路
unsuitable *adj.* 不合适的

leather bag my mother had given me, and a silver-handled ***whip***—also a gift. These did not exactly suit the rough blue blanket and tin coffee pot I carried with them. To my embarrassment, my revolver would not stay properly in its ***holster*** at my side. It kept working its way around to where it hung down in front.

I was too proud to arrive at Jim's door ***penniless***, so I didn't stop at any hotels along the way. I ate my gingerbread and camped out in the woods. The loneliness I felt once or twice along the road completely disappeared in the sweet and silent ***companionship*** of the woods. I wasn't aware of hunger, and I slept soundly, quite forgetting the pain of my blistered feet. In the morning I found I had emptied my water bottle. I also found I had completely overlooked the first rule of camping—to settle near water. But I chewed some unboiled coffee beans for breakfast, and again took up the trail.

有一根银柄皮鞭——也是别人送的礼物。这些东西跟我同时携带的粗糙的蓝毯子和锡制咖啡壶不是很匹配。令我尴尬的是，左轮手枪放在腰间的枪套里大小不是很合适。它总是在里面乱咣，最后从前面耷拉下来。

自尊心不允许我身无分文地去见吉姆，所以，一路上不敢在任何旅店歇脚。我饿了就啃那块姜饼，困了就在树林里露营。有一两次在路上觉得孤独，一进到林子里，有芬芳的、无声的树木陪伴，那种孤独感就完全消失了。我并不觉得饥饿，睡得也香甜，几乎忘记了脚上水泡的疼痛。早上，我发现瓶子里的水喝光了。我还发现我已经完全忽略了野营的首要规则——近水安营。但嚼了一些生咖啡豆当早餐后，就继续走小路。

---

whip *n.* 鞭子
holster *n.* 手枪皮套
penniless *adj.* 身无分文的
companionship *n.* 友谊

The pine-filled air, the distant view of mountains, led me onward. I was excited to see strange, white pieces of rock, shining like teeth against the red dirt. This was called ***quartz***, I had been told. Quartz was a sign of a gold mining district. At about sunset I came out of the pines and looked across at a mountain side covered with white tents. They stuck up out of the earth like the white quartz. It was the "diggings"!

I do not know what I had expected, but I was ***disappointed***. As I looked across at the mining camp, the sun set. A great shadow covered the tents, and a number of ***tiny*** lights, like stars, shone in their place. A cold wind rushed down the ***mountainside***. I felt cold in my clothes, wet from a long day's journey. It was nine o'clock when I reached the mining camp. I had been on my feet since sunrise. But I hid my belongings in the bushes, and washed my feet in a stream

---

充满松香气味的空气，还有山峦的远景引导我向前。见到奇怪的、白色的岩石，在红土的衬托下，像牙齿一样闪闪发光，我很兴奋。有人告诉我说这种岩石叫石英。如果在什么地方发现了石英就预示着这里有金子。几近日落时分，我走出松林，向对面布满帐篷的山坡瞭望。它们像白色的石英一样从地上拔地而起。这就是矿区营地！

我不知道自己在期待着什么，但此刻感到很失望。就在我瞭望矿区营地的时候，太阳落山了。巨大的阴影笼罩了帐篷，帐篷里闪出了星星点点的灯火，看上去很像天上的星星。一股冷风从山坡上刮过，我感觉浑身发冷。走了一整天，身上穿的衣服都已经湿了。到达营地时已是九点。我从日出开始一直在走路。把身上带的东西藏在树丛里，又在溪水里洗了脚。受虚荣心的

---

quartz *n.* 石英

disappointed *adj.* 失望的

tiny *adj.* 微小的

mountainside *n.* 山腰；山坡

of water. I put on my terrible leather shoes and limped, in my painful pride, to the first miner's log ***cabin***. Here I learned that Jim was one of four partners who worked a claim two miles away, on the other side of the mountain. There was nothing for me to do but go on. I would find the Magnolia Hotel. I would buy the cheapest food, rest an hour, and then limp painfully, as best I could, to Jim's claim.

II

The Magnolia Hotel was a large wooden building. The greater part was given over to a huge drinking ***saloon***. Shining mirrors hung on the walls, and a long bar ran down one side of the room. In the unimportant dining room I ordered fish-balls and coffee because they were cheap and quick. The waiter told me that my friend Jim might live in the settlement. The ***barkeeper***, though, knew everything

---

驱使，又穿上那双可怕的皮鞋，忍着疼痛，跛着脚走向第一座矿区小木屋。一打听，才知道吉姆跟另外三个人合伙干，他们在两英里外另一座山坡上圈了自己的地盘。我只能继续上路。我要找到木兰旅馆，在那里买最廉价的食物，歇上一小时，然后尽可能忍着疼痛，跛着脚向吉姆的地盘进发。

II

木兰旅馆是一座高大的木制建筑，其中大部分都用作酒吧间。酒吧间很宽敞，墙上挂着明晃晃的镜子，房间的一侧有个长形的吧台。在那间不起眼的餐厅里，我要了炸鱼丸和咖啡，因为这两样东西价格便宜，上得也快。侍者告诉我说吉姆可能住在移民社区里。不过，酒吧老板什么事都知道，什么

---

cabin *n.* 小屋；茅屋

saloon *n.* 酒吧

barkeeper *n.* 酒吧老板

and everybody, and would tell me the shortest way to his log cabin.

I was very tired. I'm afraid I took a longer time over my food than was proper. Then I went into the saloon. It was crowded with miners and traders and a few well-dressed ***businessmen***. Here again my pride led me to ***extravagance***. I was ***ashamed*** to ask the important, white-shirted and diamond-pinned barkeeper for information, without buying a drink. I'm afraid I laid down another quarter on the bar. I asked my question, and the barkeeper passed me a bottle and glass. Suddenly a strange thing happened. As it had some effect on my future, I will tell you about it here.

The ***ceiling*** of the saloon was held up by a half-dozen tall wooden posts. They stood in front of the bar, about two feet from it. The front of the bar was crowded with drinkers. Suddenly, to my surprise,

---

人都认识，他会告诉我去吉姆小木屋最近的路。

我疲惫不堪，所以用餐的时间恐怕就比正常情况长了一些。用餐之后，我进了酒吧间。这里挤满了淘金的、做买卖的和几个衣着考究的生意人。这时，我的虚荣劲儿又上来了。对于这样重要的穿白衬衫戴钻石的酒吧老板，我羞于不买一杯啤酒就开口打听消息。我在吧台上放了二十五美分，便开口提问题。老板递给我一瓶酒和一个酒杯。这时，突然发生了一桩奇怪的事件。因为这事对我的前途产生了一些影响，所以，在此我得说说。

酒吧间的天花板是由六根高大的木桩支撑的。这些木桩就立在吧台前面大约两英尺的地方。吧台前挤满了喝酒的人。突然，他们全都放下酒杯，匆

---

businessman *n.* 商人
extravagance *n.* 奢侈；浪费
ashamed *adj.* 羞愧的
ceiling *n.* 天花板

they all put down their glasses and hurriedly backed into the spaces behind the ***posts***. At the same moment a shot was fired through the large open doors that opened into the saloon.

The bullet hit the bar and broke off pieces of wood. The shot was returned from the upper end of the bar. And then for the first time I ***realized*** that two men with revolvers were shooting at each other across the saloon.

The other men were hiding behind the posts; the barkeeper was down behind the bar. Six shots were fired by the revolvers. As far as I could see nobody was hurt. A mirror was broken, and my glass had been ***hit*** by the third shot. But the whole thing passed so quickly, and I was so surprised by it all, that I cannot remember feeling afraid. My only worry was that I would ***show*** to the others my

---

匆躲到木桩后面去了，这让我感到非常吃惊。与此同时，从通往酒吧间的敞开的大门射进一发子弹。

子弹击中了吧台，击碎一些木头。吧台另一端有人回击。这时我才第一次意识到有两个手握左轮手枪的人穿过酒吧间在对射。

另一个人躲在木桩后面，酒吧老板趴在吧台底下。两支手枪共射出六发子弹。就我所见到的，没有什么人受伤。有一面镜子被击碎了，我的酒杯被第三发子弹击中。整个事件瞬间就结束了。我过于吃惊，不记得当时有什么害怕的感觉。唯一的担忧就是别人会看出我年轻、没有经验或被吓着了。我

---

post *n.* 柱；桩
hit *v.* 击；打击
realize *v.* 认识到；了解
show *v.* 显示

youth, inexperience, or shock. I think any shy, proud young man will understand this, and would probably feel as I did. So strong was this feeling that while the smell of the ***gunpowder*** was still in my nose, I spoke out. I picked up the broken glass, and said to the barkeeper slowly, coolly, "Will you please fill me another glass? It's not my fault if this one was broken."

The barkeeper stood up behind the bar. His face was red and excited. He gave me a strange smile and passed me the bottle and a fresh glass. I heard a laugh behind me, and was embarrassed. I took a large ***gulp*** of the ***fiery*** drink and hurried to leave. But my blistered feet hurt, and I could only ***limp*** to the door. I felt a hand on my back. A voice said quickly,"You're not hurt, old man?" I recognized the man who had laughed. My face felt hot and red. I answered quickly

---

想，任何一个害羞的、骄傲的年轻人都明白这一点，也都会与我有同感。这种感觉是那样强烈，以至硝烟还还没散去，我就开口说话了。我捡起击碎的玻璃杯，缓缓地、镇定自若地对老板说：“能请你再给我倒一杯酒吗？要说这杯给击碎了，那可不是我的错。”

老板从吧台后站起身来。他的脸色红红的，很是激动。朝我奇怪地笑了笑，递给我酒瓶和一个新酒杯。我听到背后有人笑，觉得很尴尬，喝了一大口就匆匆离开了。但起泡的双脚非常疼痛，所以只能跛着脚朝门口走去。这时，我觉得有一只手搭在后背上。一个声音很快地说：“你没伤着吧，伙计？”我认出就是刚才笑的那人。我面红耳赤，急忙回答说走了远路，脚起

---

gunpowder *n.* 火药
gulp *n.* 吞咽；一大口
fiery *adj.* 辛辣的；味道强烈的
limp *v.* 跛行

that my feet were blistered from a long walk. I was in a hurry to get to Jim's claim.

"Hold on," said the stranger. He went out to the street and called to a man in a horse and wagon. "Drop him," he said, pointing at me, "at Jim's cabin, and then come back here." Then he helped me into the wagon. He ***slapped*** me on the back, and said ***mysteriously***, "You'll do!" Then he returned quickly to the saloon.

I learned from the driver about the gun fight. Two men had had a wild ***argument*** the week before. They had ***sworn*** to shoot each other "on sight"—that is, at their next meeting. They were going around with revolvers ready. The driver added that the men seemed to be "pretty bad shooters." And I, knowing nothing of these deadly weapons, and thinking pretty much what he thought, agreed! I said nothing

---

泡了。说完，就要赶紧去找吉姆。

“等一下，”那个陌生人说。他跑到大街上对一个赶着马车的人说：“把他带到吉姆的地盘上，”他指着我说，“然后再回到这儿来。”说完，帮我上了马车。他拍拍我的后背，神秘地说：“你能行！”说完，又很快地返回酒吧间了。

我从车夫那了解到这场枪战的原委。那两个人在一星期前发生了激烈的争执。他们发誓要“见面就射”——也就是，下次一见面就相互射击。不管走到哪儿，都把枪准备好。车夫还补充说，那两个人的枪法看起来真是“太糟糕”了。而我呢，因为对这些致命的武器一无所知，而且也很重视他的看法，居然表示赞同！不过，我没有谈自己的感受，并且很快就把这事给忘

---

slap *v.* 掌击；拍击

mysteriously *adv.* 神秘地

argument *n.* 争吵

swear *v.* 发誓

of my own feelings, though, and soon forgot them. For as we came near to Jim's log cabin, I had reached the end of my *journey*.

III

Now, for the first time I began to have doubts about my plan: to ask help and advice from a man I hardly knew. I believe it is a common experience of youth that during the journey I had never felt doubts. But now, as I arrived, my youth and *inexperience* came to me like a shock. And it was followed by a greater one. When at last I left my driver and entered the small log cabin, Jim's partners told me that he had left the *partnership* and gone back to San Francisco.

Perhaps I looked tired and disappointed. One of the partners pulled out the only chair and offered me a drink. With *encouragement*, I limped through my story. I think I told the exact truth. I was even

---

了。因为快到吉姆住地了，我已经到达了目的地。

III

此刻，我才第一次怀疑起我的打算：向一个几乎不认识的人请求帮助和忠告。在旅途中一直没有产生这种疑虑，我想年轻人都有过这种经历。而此刻，在我终于来到这里的时候，却一下子想到自己年轻幼稚、缺乏经验。紧接着就遇到一个更严重的问题。当最后告别车夫走进那间小木屋时，吉姆的合伙人告诉我，吉姆已经撤伙回旧金山了。

大概是因为我看上去又累又失望吧，其中一个合伙人把唯一的椅子拉过来让我坐下，还倒了一杯水。我受到了鼓励，便吃力地讲述了自己的经历。

---

journey *n.* 旅程

inexperience *n.* 缺乏经验

partnership *n.* 合伙人身份；伙伴关系

encouragement *n.* 鼓励

too tired to make it sound as if Jim and I were really friends.

They listened without speaking. Probably they had heard such stories before. I expect they had gone through a harder experience than mine. Then something happened that I am sure could have happened only in California in that time of ***simplicity*** and ***confidence***. Without a word of discussion among themselves, without a word to ask about my ***character*** or experience, they offered me Jim's partnership, "to try."

I went to bed that night in Jim's ***bunk bed***. I was one-fourth owner of a log cabin and a claim I knew nothing about. I looked around me at the four bearded faces, only a few years older than I. I wondered if we were playing at being miners as I had played at being a

---

我想我讲的都是绝对的实话。甚至连费脑筋琢磨怎样说才能让他们觉得我和吉姆是真正的朋友的力气也没有。

他们一言不发地听着。也许以前听过这类故事吧。我料想他们有过比我更难的经历。这时，出现了一件非常意外的事情。我敢肯定，这种事情只有在加州，而且是在人际关系十分简单又充满信任的那个年代才有可能发生。他们之间一句也没有商量，也一句没有询问我的人品或经历，就把吉姆的股份让给我"试一试"。

那天晚上我就在吉姆的床铺上睡了。我现在成了一个小木屋和一块我还一无所知的地盘的四个主人之一了。我环顾身边这三张长着胡须的面孔，他

---

simplicity *n.* 简单
confidence *n.* 信心；信任
character *n.* 性格；品质
bunk bed 双层床的上铺或下铺

schoolmaster.

I awoke late the next morning and stared around the empty ***cabin***. I could hardly believe that what had happened the night before wasn't a dream. The cabin was made of pine logs with four bunk beds on two sides. Bright sunlight streamed in through holes in the walls. There was a table and chair, and three old boxes for ***furniture***. There was one window beside the open door, and a ***fireplace*** at the other end. I was wondering if I had moved into an empty cabin, when my partners entered. They had let me sleep—It was twelve o'clock! My breakfast was ready. They had something funny to tell me—I was a ***hero***!

My behavior during the shooting match at the Magnolia saloon

们比我大不了几岁。我不知道自己是否像当小学教师那样，闹着玩儿似的，又当上了矿工。

第二天早晨，我很晚才醒来。环顾着空无一人的小屋，简直不敢相信昨晚发生的一切，以为是一场梦。小屋是用松木搭建的，有四张床，分别摆放在两边。明亮的阳光从墙壁的漏洞流泻进来。屋里有一张桌子、一把椅子和三个做家具用的旧箱子。在敞开的门旁边，有一扇窗户，对面还有个壁炉。我正纳闷自己是不是搬进一个空屋子来了，这时，那些合伙人进来了。他们让我睡足了——已经十二点了！早餐已经准备好了。他们还有一件有趣的事要告诉我——我成了英雄！

我在木兰酒吧间射击现场的表现被当时在场的人谈论得热火朝天，传诵

---

cabin *n.* 小屋　　furniture *n.* 家具

fireplace *n.* 壁炉　　hero *n.* 英雄

was being discussed and reported by men who had been there. The story was wildly ***enlarged***. They said I had stood coolly at the bar, quietly demanding a drink while the shots were being fired!I told my partners the truth, but I am afraid they didn't believe me. They thought I was young enough to be embarrassed by being noticed, and they changed the ***subject***.

Yes, they said, I could go digging that day. Where? Oh, anywhere on ground that was not already claimed. There were hundreds of square miles to choose from. How to do it? You mean, you have never mined before? Never dug for gold at all? Never! I saw them look quickly at each other. My heart ***sank***. But I noticed that their eyes were bright and happy. Then I learned that my inexperience was considered lucky. Gold miners believed in "beginner's luck," the

---

得沸沸扬扬。整个儿事情被无限地夸大了。他们说我当时镇定自若地站在吧台边，就在双方对射的当口，平静地要求老板还我一杯酒！我把实情告诉给这些合伙人，但我觉得他们不相信。他们认为我因为年轻，不好意思受人瞩目，于是就换了话题。

他们同意我当天就去淘金。在哪儿？哦，随便哪个地方都行，只要是还没有被别人圈定。方圆数百英里的地方随便挑选。怎样挑选呢？你的意思是，你以前从来没有淘过什么吗？从来没有淘过金吗？从来没有！我看到他们很快地互相看了一眼。我的心往下一沉。但又注意到他们的眼睛闪着快乐

---

enlarge *v.* 扩大；详述

subject *n.* 话题

sink *v.* 下沉

unexplained luck that came to first-time miners. But I must choose a place to dig myself, to make the luck work.

I was given a pick and *shovel*, and a pan to wash the gold *nuggets* from the dirt. I decided to dig on a *grassy* hillside about two hundred yards from the cabin. They told me to fill my pan with dirt around a large area. In one or two shovels-full I dug up some pieces of shining quartz, and put them hopefully in my pocket. Then I filled my pan. I carried it with difficulty—it was *surprisingly* heavy—to the stream to wash it. As I moved the pan back and forth in the running water, the red dirt washed away. Only stones and black sand were left. I picked out the stones with my fingers, and kept only a small flat, pretty, round stone. It looked like a coin. I put it in my pocket with the quartz. Then I washed away the black sand. You can imagine how I

的光芒。接着，我才知道没干过淘金倒是一件好事，被认为是幸运。他们相信“新手的运气”，那是一种来自初次淘金者的无法解释的运气。但必须选一个地方自己挖，这样，“运气”才能奏效。

他们给了我一把镐、一把铲，还有一个淘金盘，是用来从泥土里筛洗天然金块的。我决定在离住地两百码远的长满青草的山坡上开挖。他们告诉我要大面积取土，把盘子装满。我挖了一两铲就挖出一些闪光的石英。我满怀希望地把石英装进衣袋里。接着，又挖土装盘。装满了一盘后，我又吃力地——想不到这东西这么重——把它端到河里冲洗。在流水里来回摇动盘子，红土被冲走了，只剩下了石子和黑沙。我把石子都挑出去，只留下一块扁平的、样子很漂亮的小圆石子，看上去像一块硬币。我把它揣进衣袋里跟

---

shovel *n.* 铁铲

nugget *n.* 天然金块；矿石

grassy *adj.* 长满草的

surprisingly *adv.* 惊人地

felt when I saw a ***dozen*** tiny gold stars in the bottom of the pan! They were so small that I was afraid I would wash them away. I learned later that they are so heavy that there is very little danger of that. I ran happily to where my partners were working.

"Yes, he's got the 'color,'" one said without excitement. "I knew it."

I was disappointed. "Then I haven't struck gold?" I said shyly.

"Not in this pan. You've only got a quarter of a dollar there. But," he continued with a smile, "you only have to get that much in four pans, and you've made enough for your ***daily*** food."

石英放在一起。接着，又把黑沙冲掉了。你可以想象，当我看到盘底有十几粒微小的金星时有多么兴奋！它们太小了，我担心一不小心就会被冲走。后来我才知道它们很重不大可能有这种危险。我高兴地跑到合伙人干活的地方。

"是啊，他已经见到'微粒'了，我认识这东西。"一个人说，听声音，他并没有显示出激动。

我失望了。"这么说，我找的不是金子？"我害羞地说。

"不在这盘里。这些仅值25美分。但是，"他仍然笑着说，"得弄四盘这样的东西，才够你一天吃的。"

---

dozen *n.* 十二个；一打

daily *adj.* 日常的

"And that's all any of us—or anyone on this claim—have made in the last six months!" another partner said.

This was another shock to me. But he spoke with good humor and youthful ***carelessness***. I took comfort from that. But I was still disappointed by my first try. I shyly pulled the quartz out of my pocket.

"I found these," I said. "They look as if they have gold in them. See how it shines?"

My partner smiled. "That's ***worthless***. Those are iron ***pyrites***, called 'fool's gold.' But what's that?" he added quickly. He took the round flat stone from my hand, "Where did you find that?"

"那也是我们所有的人——或者说，是这块地盘上所有的人——这六个月来所淘到的全部！"另一个人说。

这话又让我吃了一惊。但是，就因为他说话的口气很幽默，也有一种年轻人满不在乎的神气，我才从中得到了些许安慰。但仍然为自己的初试感到失望。我羞怯地从衣袋里掏出石英。

"我发现了这些东西，"我说。"看样子这里含有金子。看到它在闪光了吧？"

我的合伙人笑了。"这不值钱，是硫化铁矿，人称'傻瓜'的金子。可那是什么？"他又很快地加了一句。他把那个扁圆的石头从我手里接过去。"这是从哪儿弄的？"

---

carelessness *n.* 粗心大意；漫不经心

worthless *adj.* 不值钱的

pyrite *n.* 黄铁矿

"In the same hole as the quartz. Is it good for anything?"

He did not answer, but turning to the other partners who were coming over to see, he said, "Look!"

He laid my stone on another stone and hit it with his ***pick***. I was surprised that it didn't break. Where the pick had hit it, it showed a bright yellow star!

I had no time, or need, to ask another question. "Write out a claim notice!" he said to one partner. And, "Run, get a post!" to the other. We put the notice on the post, to ***announce*** our claim, and began to dig ***madly***.

"跟石英一块儿挖出来的。有什么用吗？"

他没有回答，却转身对那两个正在过来看的人说："看！"

他把我的石头放在另一块石头上，用镐去砸。没有砸碎，我感到很吃惊。在镐头砸中的地方闪出一颗明亮的黄星！

我没时间，也没必要再问什么了。"赶快写个占地告示！"他对一个合伙人说。然后，又对另一个说："快跑，去立个柱子！"我们把告示贴到柱子上宣告这块地盘归我们所有，然后就开始疯狂地挖掘起来。

---

pick *n.* 镐

announce *v.* 宣布

madly *adj.* 疯狂地

The gold nugget I had picked up was ***worth*** about twelve dollars. We carried many pans, we worked that day and the next hopefully, happily, and without tiring. Then we worked at the claim daily, carefully, and regularly for three weeks. Sometimes we found the "color," and sometimes we didn't. But we nearly always got enough for our daily food. We laughed, joked, told stories and enjoyed ourselves as if we were at an ***endless*** picnic. But that twelve-dollar nugget was the first and last find we made on the new, "Beginner's Luck" claim!

我挖出的天然金块价值12美元。我们搬运了很多土，在当天和第二天都满怀信心地、愉快地、不知疲倦地干着。接着又在这块地盘里日复一日地、谨小慎微地、满有规律地干了三个星期。有时能够发现“微粒”，有时什么也没有。但差不多总能维持日常的伙食。我们哈哈笑着，开着玩笑，讲着故事，整天自得其乐，就好像是在享受一顿无尽的野餐。但那价值12美元的天然金块是我们第一次也是最后一次在这块新的，有着“新手运气”的地盘上挖到的宝藏！

---

worth *adj.* 值……的

endless *adj.* 无止境的

The Story of an Hour

Adapted from the story by Kate Chopin

Kate Chopin was born in 1851 in St. Louis, Missouri. Her family was rich. She married, and had six children. She lived a family life like other rich ladies in those days. But she was well *educated* and liked to read and write. After her husband died in 1883, she began to write stories. She also wrote a book called *The Awakening*. This book, and many of her stories, shocked her readers at that time. She wrote about the *freedom* of women. But at that time,

一个小时的故事

根据凯特·肖邦的同名故事改写

凯特·肖邦1851年生于密苏里州的圣路易斯，家境富有，婚后育有六个子女。她跟当时其他阔太太一样过着安居乐业的生活，但她受过良好的教育，喜欢读书和写作。丈夫1883年去世后她便开始写故事。她还写了一本名为《觉醒》的书。这本书，以及她的许多故事震撼了当时的读者。她描写女性自由，而在当时，绝大多数女性都仅仅是为各

educated *adj.* 受过……教育的

freedom *n.* 自由

most women lived only for their families. Because the stories were shocking, people did not read them for many years after her death in 1904. Now Kate Chopin's writing has been *discovered* again. People are interested in her life and work.

They knew that Louise Mallard had a weak heart. So they broke the bad news softly. Her husband, Brently, was dead.

"There was a train *accident*, Louise,"said her sister, Josephine, quietly.

Her husband's friend, Richards, stood with Josephine. Richards brought the news, but Josephine told the story. She spoke in broken sentences.

"Richards... was at the newspaper office. News of the accident came. Louise... Louise, Brently's name was on the list. Brently... was

---

自的家庭而活着。由于她的故事大逆不道，人们在她1904去世后多年不读这些作品。如今，凯特·肖邦的作品又被重新发掘出来。人们对她的生活和工作产生了兴趣。

他们知道路易丝·玛拉德心脏不好，所以在向她透露这个噩耗时谨小慎微。她的丈夫布伦特里死了。

“路易丝，听说发生了一起火车事故，”她姐姐约瑟芬平静地说。

她丈夫的朋友理查兹站在约瑟芬旁边。带来消息的是理查兹，可开口说话的是约瑟芬。她的话说得断断续续。

“理查兹……刚好在报社。传来了火车出事的消息。路易丝……路易丝，布伦特里的名字也在上面。布伦特里……死了，路易丝。”

---

discover *v.* 发现　　accident *n.* 事故

killed, Louise."

Louise did not hear the story *coldly*, like some women would. She could not close her mind or her heart to the news. Like a sudden *storm*, her tears broke out. She cried loudly in her sister's arms. Then, just as suddenly, the *tears* stopped. She went to her room alone. She wanted no one with her.

In front of the window stood an empty chair. She sat down and looked out of the window. She was very tired after her tears. Her body felt cold, her mind and heart were empty.

Outside her window she could see the trees. The air smelled like spring rain. She could hear someone singing *far away*. Birds sang near the house. Blue sky showed between the clouds. She rested.

路易丝并非像有些女人那样漠然地听着。她的心无法排斥这个消息，眼泪像突来的风暴一般奔涌而泄。她在姐姐的怀里放声大哭。哭着哭着，又突然止住了。真是说哭就哭，说停就停。她独自走进自己的房间，不想要任何人陪着。

窗前摆着一把空椅。她坐下来，朝窗外望去。刚才一场痛哭，现在觉得很累，浑身发冷，心里空落落的。

窗外的树林清晰可见。空气就像春雨过后一样清新。远处有人在唱歌。鸟儿在房子附近鸣叫。蓝蓝的天空躲在飘浮的云朵后面，时隐时现。她歇息了。

---

coldly *adv.* 冷漠地

storm *n.* 暴风雨

tear *n.* 眼泪

far away 遥远的

She sat ***quietly***, but a few weak tears still fell. She had a young, strong face. But now her eyes showed nothing. She looked out of the window at the blue sky. She was not thinking, or seeing. She was waiting.

There was something coming to her. She was waiting for it with fear. What was it? She did not know; she could not give it a name. But she felt it coming out from the sky. It reached her through the sound, the smell, the color of the air.

Slowly she became ***excited***. Her ***breath*** came fast, her heart beat faster. She began to see this thing. It wanted to find her and take her. She tried to ***fight against*** it. But she could not. Her mind was as weak as her two small white hands. Then she stopped fighting against it.

她静静地坐着，眼中仍有几滴清泪在慢慢滚落。她面容年轻而刚毅，可现在却目中无神。望着窗外的蓝天，什么也没想，什么也没看，她在等待着。

有什么东西来了，她正心怀恐惧地等着它。可它是什么呢？她不知道，那是一种无以名状的东西。她觉得那东西正在从天而降，穿过空气中的声音、气味和颜色飘然而至。

渐渐地，她开始兴奋起来。呼吸变得急促，心跳也加快了。她能看到这个东西了。它想要找到她，抓住她。她奋力抵抗，但却无济于事。她的心就跟那双白嫩的小手一样柔弱无力。于是，她不再挣扎了。一个短短的

---

quietly *adv.* 安静地

breath *n.* 呼吸

excited *adj.* 兴奋的

fight against 与……作斗争

A little word broke from her ***lips***.

"Free," she said. "Free, free, free!" The ***emptiness*** and fear left her. Her eyes showed her excitement. Her heart beat fast, and the blood warmed her body. A sudden feeling of joy excited her.

She did not stop to ask if her joy was wrong. She saw her freedom clearly. She could not stop to think of smaller things.

She knew the tears would come again when she saw her husband's body. The kind hands, now dead and still. The loving face, now still and gray. But she looked into the future. She saw many long years to come that would belong to her alone. And now she opened her arms wide to those years in welcome.

词从唇间脱口而出。

"自由，"她说。"自由，自由，自由！"空虚与恐惧顿然消失，眼里闪着兴奋的光芒。她的心在狂跳，热血温暖了周身。这突如其来的愉悦感使她兴奋不已。

她没有停顿下来反问自己是否应该高兴，她已经清清楚楚地看到了自由，顾不上那些小事儿了。

她知道，看见丈夫的遗体时还会流泪。那双亲切的大手，如今已僵死了；那亲爱的面容，也已经变得僵硬灰暗。但是放眼未来，她看到还有很多年会完全属于自己。她正张开双臂去迎接那即将到来的美好时光。

---

lip *n.* 嘴唇

emptiness *n.* 空虚

There would be no one else to live for during those years. She would live for herself alone. There would be no strong ***mind*** above hers. Men and women always believe they can tell others what to do and how to think. Suddenly Louise understood that this was wrong. She could ***break away*** and be free of it.

And yet, she loved him—sometimes. Often she did not. What did love mean now? Now she understood that freedom is stronger than love.

"Free! Body and mind free!" she said again.

Her sister, Josephine, was waiting outside the door.

"Please open the door," Josephine cried. "You will make yourself

---

在那些岁月里，她不必再为别人，而是为自己而活着。再也不会有什么意见强加于她。不论男女，人们总是认为自己有权支配别人的行为和思想。路易丝忽然明白了，这是不对的。她要冲破这种束缚，从中获得解脱。

话又说回来，她还是爱他的——在有些时候，但通常不爱。什么是爱？现在她认为自由比爱更强大。

“自由！身心都要自由！”她又说。

她的姐姐约瑟芬正在门外等着。

“请你开门，”约瑟芬喊道。“你那样会生病的。你在里面干什么

---

mind *n.* 意见；精神

break away 脱离

sick. What are you doing in there, Louise? Please, please, let me in!"

"Go away. I am not sick." No, she was drinking in life through that open window.

She thought *joyfully* of all those days before her. Spring days, summer days. *All kinds of* days that would be her own. She began to hope life would be long. And just yesterday, life seemed too long!

After a while she got up and opened the door. Her eyes were bright, her *cheeks* were red. She didn't know how strong and well she looked—so full of joy. They went downstairs, where Richards was waiting.

呢，路易丝？快点，让我进去吧！"

"你走吧，我没事。"是的，她正通过那扇敞开的窗户汲取生命力。

她愉快地想着未来所有的日子：春天、夏天，所有的日子都归自己所有。她开始期望生命能够延长。而就在昨天，生活还似乎长不可奈。

过了一会儿，她站起身来，打开房门。目光明亮，面色红润，不知道自己看起来有多健壮——简直是春光满面。她们下楼了，理查兹正在楼下等着。

---

joyfully *adv.* 高兴地；喜悦地　　all kinds of 各种各样的

cheek *n.* 面颊

A man was opening the door. It was Brently Mallard. He was dirty, and tired. He carried a ***suitcase*** and an ***umbrella***. He was not killed in the train accident. He didn't even know there was an accident. He was surprised at Josephine's sudden cry. He didn't understand why Richards moved suddenly between them, to hide Louise from her husband.

But Richards was too late.

When the doctors came, they said it was her weak heart. They said she died of joy—of joy that kills.

有人在开门。是布伦特里·玛拉德。他风尘仆仆，疲惫不堪，手里还提着一个行李箱和一把雨伞。他并没有丧身车祸。他甚至不知道有车祸发生。他对约瑟芬的惊叫感到吃惊；也不明白理查兹为什么突然快步跑到他们中间，把路易丝和自己的丈夫隔开。

可是，理查兹还是迟了。

医生来了，说是因为她心脏功能太弱。他们说是因狂喜而死——能置人于死地的狂喜。

---

suitcase *n.* 手提箱

umbrella *n.* 雨伞

The Romance of a Busy Broker

Adapted from the story by O.Henry

O.Henry was born in Greensboro, North Carolina, in 1862. His real name was William Sydney Porter. He left school at the age of fifteen and worked at different times in a ***drugstore***, a business office, a building ***designer's*** office, and finally a bank. When he was caught taking money from his own bank, he was arrested and put in prison for three years. He had begun writing, and while

股票经纪人的忙里偷闲

根据欧·亨利同名故事改写

欧·亨利1862年生于北卡罗来纳州的格林斯保罗。原名是威廉·西德尼·波特。15岁弃学，曾在杂货店、商业部门的营业室、建筑设计师办公室工作，最后又到银行。曾因挪用公款而服刑三年。在狱

drugstore *n.* 药房

designer *n.* 设计师

THE ROMANCE OF A BUSY BROKER

he was in prison he published a book of adventure stories called *Cabbages and Kings*. He moved to New York in 1902, and it was there that he became famous for his short stories with surprise endings. He wrote hundreds of stories about the ordinary people of New York City. His most famous books include *The Four Million* and *The Voice of the City*. O. Henry died in 1910.

I

Pitcher had worked for many years in the office of Harvey Maxwell, the ***stockbroker***. Pitcher was a quiet man. He didn't usually let his face show his feelings. But this morning he looked surprised—and very interested. Harvey Maxwell had arrived ***energetically*** as usual at 9:30. But this morning, the young lady who was his ***secretary*** had

---

中开始写作并发表一部历险故事集，题目是《白菜与国王》。1902年移居纽约。在那里，他因描写故事有意外的结局而闻名。欧·亨利共写了几百篇有关普通纽约市民的故事，最著名的作品包括《四百万》和《城市之声》。他逝世于1910年。

I

皮切尔已经在股票经纪人哈维·麦克斯维尔的办公室工作多年了。他一向寡言少语，性格内向，很少流露内心的喜怒哀乐。但今天早晨，却显出一副吃惊的样子，而且饶有兴致。哈维·麦克斯维尔在九点半就精神抖擞地来上班了，这倒没什么两样。所不同的是，今天早晨，那个给他当秘书的年轻女士竟是跟他一起来的！皮切尔饶有兴致地看着他们两人，而麦

---

stockbroker *n.* 股票经纪人　　energetically *adv.* 精力充沛地
secretary *n.* 秘书

arrived with him. Pitcher watched them with interest. Harvey Maxwell didn't ***pay attention to*** Pitcher. He said only a quick"Good morning," and ran to his desk. He dug energetically into the mountain of letters and ***telegrams*** that waited for him. The stockbroker's day had begun.

Miss Leslie, the young lady, had been Maxwell's secretary for a year. She was beautiful, and she dressed ***simply***. Unlike some secretaries, she never wore cheap glass jewelry. Her dress was gray and plain, but it fitted her body ***nicely***. With it she wore a small black hat with a green-gold flower at the side. This morning her face shone with happiness. Her eyes were bright, her face a soft pink.

Pitcher, still interested, noticed that she acted differently this

---

克斯维尔却没有理会他。这位老板只是很快地说了声“早晨好”，就直奔自己的办公桌，一头扎进那一大堆等候处理的信件和电报中。股票经纪人忙碌的一天就这样开始了。

那位年轻的女士莱斯莉小姐给麦克斯维尔当秘书已经有一年了。她长得很美，但衣着打扮却很简朴。从来不像某些女秘书那样佩戴廉价的玻璃首饰。她的服装，格调虽然素淡，但穿在身上却显得优雅得体，再配上一顶小黑帽，帽子旁边还别着一朵黄中透绿的小花儿，更显得超凡脱俗。今天早晨，她满面春风地走来，目光神采奕奕，面颊柔美红润。

皮切尔兴致不减，他注意到她今天早晨的举止不同以往。往常她总是

---

pay attention to 注意

telegram *n.* 电报

simply *adv.* 朴素地

nicely *adv.* 漂亮地

morning. Usually she walked straight inside to her own desk. But this morning she stayed in the outside office. She walked over near Maxwell's desk. Maxwell didn't seem to be a man anymore. He had changed into a busy New York stockbroker. He'd become a *machine* of many moving parts.

"Well—what is it? Is anything wrong?" Maxwell asked his secretary. He wasn't looking at her. His eyes were on his *mail*. Letters and telegrams lay on his desk like snow.

"It's nothing," she said softly. She *moved away* with a little smile. "Mr. Pitcher," she said, coming over to him, "did Mr. Maxwell ask you to *hire* another secretary yesterday?"

径直走进里间到自己的办公桌去，而今天早晨，却留在外面没有进去。她朝麦克斯维尔的办公桌走去，而此时的麦克斯维尔已经不再是个正常的人了，已变成了一个忙碌的纽约股票经纪人，变成了一台有着许多活动部件的机器。

“喔，怎么了？有什么不对头的吗？”麦克斯维尔问他的秘书。他说这话时并没有抬头看她，而是盯着手里的邮件。那些信件和电报像雪片一样堆在桌上。

莱斯莉温柔地说，“没事儿”。说完就微笑着走开了。她走到皮切尔面前，问道：“皮切尔先生，昨天麦克斯维尔先生有没有让再雇一个秘书？”

---

machine *n.* 机械；机器
mail *n.* 邮件
move away 离开
hire *v.* 雇用

"Yes, he did," answered Pitcher. "He told me to get another one. I asked the secretarial school to send over a few this morning. But it's 9:45, and no one has come yet."

"I will do the work ***as usual***, then," said the young lady, "until someone comes to fill the place." And she went to her desk at once. She ***hung up*** the black hat with the green-gold flower in its usual place.

Harvey Maxwell was always a busy stockbroker, but today he was even busier than usual. The ***ticker*** tape machine began to throw out tape. The desk telephone began to ring. Men crowded into the office, buying and selling, crying and ***yelling***. Boys ran in and out with telegrams. Even Pitcher's face looked more alive. Maxwell

---

"有啊，"皮切尔说。"他让我再雇一个秘书，我让秘书学校今天派几个过来，可现在都9:45了，却一个也没来。"

年轻的女士说："那好吧，在别人接替之前，我还像往常一样干吧。"她马上走到自己桌前，把那顶别着黄花的黑帽子挂到了平时常挂的地方。

哈维·麦克斯维尔一直就是个忙忙碌碌的股票经纪人，今天更是忙得不可开交。办公室里自动收报机开始收报，桌上的电话骤然响起，人们一拥而入，买声、卖声、喊声、叫声不绝于耳。送电报的跑进跑出，忙个不停。就连皮切尔的表情也不那么呆板了。麦克斯维尔一把把椅子推到墙

---

as usual 像往常一样

hang up 悬挂

ticker *n.* 自动收报机

yell *v.* 叫喊

pushed his chair against the wall. He ran energetically from ticker tape to telephone, jumping like a dancer.

In the middle of all this action and yelling, the stockbroker realized that someone new had arrived. He first saw a high mountain of golden hair under a large round hat. Then he ***noticed*** some large glass jewelry. Underneath all this was a young lady. Pitcher saw that Maxwell didn't know who she was. He came forward to ***explain***. "Here is the lady from the secretarial school," Pitcher said to Maxwell. "She came for the job."

Maxwell turned around with his hands full of papers and ticker tape. "What job?" he yelled. His face looked ***angry***.

"The secretarial job," Pitcher said quietly. "You told me yesterday

---

边，从收报机到电话机之间穿梭往来，忙得不亦乐乎，真像个舞蹈演员在表演舞蹈。

我们这位股票经纪人正忙得一塌糊涂，这时，却突然发觉面前站了个生人儿。他首先看到的是一顶阔边圆帽下高高绾起的金发，然后又注意到一件硕大的玻璃首饰。最后才看到这些东西下面的人，是一位年轻的女士。皮切尔看出麦克斯维尔不认识她，忙上前解释道：“她是秘书学校派来应聘那份工作的。”

麦克斯维尔转过身，手里握着一大堆收报机输出的纸条。“什么工作?”他叫喊着，面带愠色。

“秘书，”皮切尔平静地说：“你昨天不是告诉我给秘书学校打电话

---

push *v.* 推动
notice *v.* 注意到
explain *v.* 说明；解释
angry *adj.* 生气的

to call the school. I asked them to send one over this morning."

"You're losing your mind, Pitcher! Why would I tell you a thing like that? Miss Leslie has worked well for a whole year here. The job is hers while she wants to stay. There is no job here, Madam! Tell the secretarial school, Pitcher. Don't bring any more of them in here!"

The lady turned to leave. Her hat almost ***hit*** Pitcher in the eye as she ***angrily*** walked past him out of the office. Pitcher thought to himself that Maxwell was getting more ***forgetful*** every day.

II

The office became busier and busier. Orders to buy and sell came and went like birds flying. Maxwell ***was worried about*** his own stocks, too, and worked faster and harder. This was the stock market, the

---

吗？我让他们今天上午派一个过来。"

"你疯了，皮切尔！我怎么会让你干这种事儿？莱斯莉小姐在这儿干一整年了，她干得好好的，只要她愿意，这工作就是她的。女士，这里没你的工作！皮切尔，告诉秘书学校以后别再往这儿派人了！"

那女士一听，转身就走。就在从皮切尔身边经过时，她的帽子差点撞着皮切尔的眼睛。皮切尔暗自思忖着：这老板可是一天比一天健忘了。

II

办公室里越来越忙乱了。收进和出手的指令就像一窝蜂一样乱哄哄地飞来飞去。麦克斯维尔也在担心自己的股票，所以干得更快，也更猛了。

---

hit *v.* 碰撞

angrily *adv.* 愤怒地

forgetful *adj.* 健忘的

be worried about 担心

world of money. There was no room in it for the world of human feelings or the world of ***nature***.

Near lunchtime, everything ***quieted down***. Maxwell stood by his desk with his hands full of telegrams. His pen was behind his ear. His hair stood up on his head. Suddenly through the open window came a smell of flowers, like the thin breath of spring. Maxwell stood still. This was Miss Leslie's smell, her own and only hers. The smell seemed to bring her before him. The world of the stock market ***disappeared***. And Miss Leslie was in the next room—only twenty steps away.

"I'll do it now," said Maxwell softly. "I'll ask her now. Why didn't I do it long ago?"

这就是股票市场，金钱的世界。在这个世界里，人类的情感世界和其他的一切都是无处容身的。

快到吃午饭的时候，一切喧嚣都渐渐平息下来。麦克斯维尔站在桌边，手里全是电报，耳后还别着钢笔，头发根根倒竖。突然间，透过开着的窗子，飘来一阵花香，宛如春天那纤柔的呼吸。麦克斯维尔静静地站在那里。这是莱斯莉小姐的味道，是她独有的味道。这味道仿佛把她带到了他的面前。一瞬间，股票市场的一切都消失得无影无踪，莱斯莉小姐就在隔壁——仅20步之隔。

"我现在就办，"麦克斯维尔轻轻地说。"我现在就问她。为什么不早说呢？"

---

nature *n.* 自然

quiet down 安静下来

disappear *v.* 消失

He ran into her office. He jumped towards her desk. She looked up at him with a smile. Her face turned a soft pink. Her eyes were kind. Maxwell put his hands on her desk. They were still full of papers.

"Miss Leslie," he said, hurrying, "I only have a ***moment*** to talk. I want to say something important in that moment: Will you be my wife? I haven't had time to show you, but I really do love you. Speak quickly please—there's the telephone."

"Why—what are you talking about?" cried the young lady. She stood up and looked at him ***strangely***.

"Don't you understand?" Maxwell asked quickly, looking back

他冲进她的办公室，一个箭步跳到她的桌前。她抬起头来，面带微笑，脸颊绯红，目光亲切。麦克斯维尔把双手放到她的桌子上，手中仍然握着那些电报。

"莱斯莉小姐，"他急切地说："我只有这么一点点时间跟你说话，我得充分利用这点时间和你说件重要的事：你愿意嫁给我吗？我没有时间向你表白，但我确实是真心爱你。请马上答应我——你看又来电话了。"

"什么？你说什么？"年轻的女士惊呼起来。站起身来，非常奇怪地看着他。

"你不明白吗？"麦克斯维尔一边很快地问，一边回头看自己桌上的

---

moment *n.* 片刻；一会儿　　　strangely *adv.* 奇怪地

at the phone on his desk. "I want you to marry me. I've ***stolen*** this moment to ask you, now, while things have quieted down a little. Take the telephone, Pitcher!" he yelled. "Will you, Miss Leslie?" he ***added*** softly.

The secretary acted very strange. At first she seemed surprised. Then she began to cry. But then she smiled through her tears like the sun through rain. She put her arm around the stockbroker's neck.

"I know now," she said. "It's this business that put it out of your head. I was afraid, at first. But don't you remember, Harvey? We were married last evening at 8:00, in the little church around the corner."

电话。"我要你嫁给我。我这是趁这会儿都安静了，忙里偷闲向你求婚。接电话，皮切尔！"他喊道。"你愿意吗，莱斯莉小姐？"他又充满柔情地补充了一句。

我们这位秘书的反应非常奇怪。起初，她看上去很吃惊，接着就哭了。但很快又破涕为笑，那笑容就像雨后的阳光一样灿烂。她张开双臂，搂住股票经纪人的脖子。

"现在我明白了，"她说，"是这股票生意让你忙晕了头。刚才可真把我给吓着了。可是，哈维，难道你真的不记得了吗？昨天晚上八点，就在街角的那个小教堂里，我们不是已经结婚了吗？"

---

steal *v.* 偷窃

add *v.* 补充说

A Day's Wait

Adapted from the story by Ernest Hemingway

Ernest Hemingway was born in Oak Park, Illinois in 1899. His father, a doctor, ***encouraged*** his love of the outdoor life of camping, fishing, and hunting. As a boy he spent summer ***vacations*** in the woods of upper Michigan, which later became the setting for some of his best-known stories. In World War I, Hemingway offered his services as a Red Cross ***ambulance*** driver, and in 1918 he was

---

一天的等待

根据欧内思特·海明威同名故事改写

欧内思特·海明威1899年生于伊利诺伊州的橡树园。父亲是一位医生，他鼓励儿子热爱野营、垂钓和打猎等户外活动。童年时期，海明威就在密歇根北部的树林里度过一个个暑假，这种生活经历后来成了他的某些名著的写作背景。在第一次世界大战中，海明威在红十字救护队服役，当司机。1918年，他在意大利身负重伤。他的三部最佳小

---

encourage *v.* 鼓励
vacation *n.* 假期
ambulance *n.* 救护车

A DAY'S WAIT

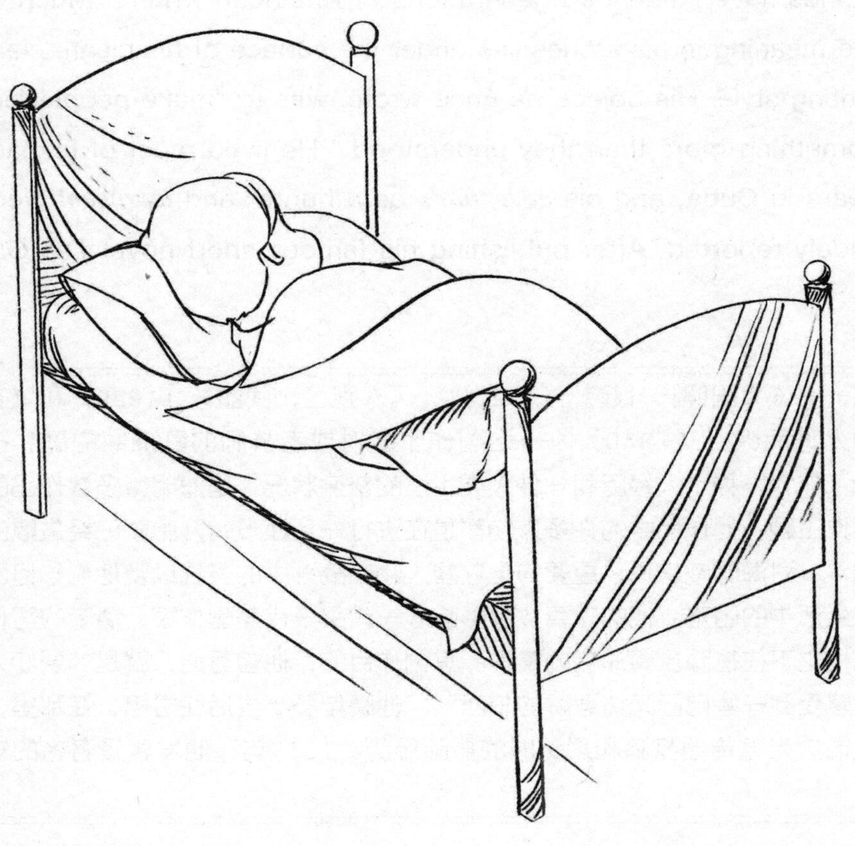

seriously wounded in Italy. Three of his best ***novels***—*The Sun Also Rises* (1926), *A Farewell to Arms* (1929), and *For Whom the Bell Tolls* (1940)—take place in Europe during or after a war. Indeed, war, as a personal experience and as a general condition of human life, is central to most of Hemingway's writing. Many of his ***characters*** are fighting a battle that was lost before they began fighting. What is important to Hemingway is the way the characters behave in that battle and how they face the difficulties of life. Hemingway's short stories have influenced generations of American writers. Much of the meaning in his stories lies under the surface of his clean, clear writing style. His object, he once wrote, was to "make people feel something more than they understood." He lived most of his last years in Cuba, and his ***adventures*** as a hunter and ***journalist*** were widely reported. After publishing his famous short novel *The Old*

说——《太阳照样升起》（1926）、《永别了，武器》（1929）和《丧钟为谁而鸣》（1940）——均创作于战时或者战后的欧洲。的确，战争，作为一种个人经历和一种人类生活的普遍状况，是海明威多数作品的创作主题。他作品中的许多人物都是在进行一场还没有开始就已经失败的战斗。对海明威来说，重要的是这些人物在战斗中的表现以及他们如何面对生活中的困难。他的短篇故事影响了一代又一代美国作家，清晰的写作风格之下往往隐含着深刻的寓意。其创作目的，他曾写道，就是“要使人们感受到一些自己无法理解的东西”。他晚年多半生活在古巴，在那里，人们广为宣传他打猎和采访时的冒险经历。1952年，他发表了著名的短

novel *n.* 小说
character *n.* 角色
adventure *n.* 冒险
journalist *n.* 新闻工作者

Man and the Sea in 1952, Hemingway was awarded the Pulitzer Prize (1953) and the Nobel Prize for ***literature*** (1954). He left Cuba in 1960, moved to Idaho, and in 1961 ended his own life by shooting himself.

He came into the room to ***shut*** the windows while we were still in bed and I saw he looked ill. He was ***shivering***, his face was white, and he walked slowly as though it ached to move.

"What's the matter, ***Schatz***?"

"I've got a headache."

"You better go back to bed."

"No. I'm all right."

"You go to bed. I'll see you when I'm dressed."

篇小说《老人与海》，此后，荣获普力策奖（1953），并于1954年荣获诺贝尔文学奖。1960年，他离开古巴，移居爱达荷州。1961年，开枪结束了自己的生命。

他走进我们房间关窗户的时候，我们还没起床。我见他一副病容，全身哆嗦，脸色苍白，步履艰难，好像每迈一步都会引起疼痛。

"怎么啦，宝贝？"

"我头痛。"

"你最好再回床上去躺一会儿。"

"不，我没事儿。"

"你先去躺一会儿，我穿好衣服就去看你。"

---

literature *n.* 文学
shut *v.* 关；闭
shiver *v.* 颤抖；哆嗦
schatz *n.* [德语]心肝；宝贝

But when I came downstairs he was dressed, sitting by the fire, looking a very sick and ***miserable*** boy of nine years. When I put my hand on his ***forehead*** I knew he had a fever.

"You go up to bed," I said, "you're sick."

"I'm all right," he said.

When the doctor came he took the boy's temperature.

"What is it?" I asked him.

"One hundred and two."

Downstairs, the doctor left three different medicines in different colored ***capsules*** with instructions for giving them. One was to bring down the fever, another a ***purgative***, the third to overcome an acid condition. The germs of influenza can only exist in an acid condition,

---

可是当我下楼时，他已经穿好了衣服，坐在炉边。他才9岁啊，看上去病得很厉害，一副让人可怜的样子。我用手摸摸他的额头，知道他发烧了。

“你到楼上去躺着，”我说，“你病了。”

“我没病，”他说。

医生来后，量了孩子的体温。

“多少度？”我问医生。

“102度。”

下楼后，医生留下三种药，其胶囊的颜色各不相同，并下了医嘱。第一种是退烧药，另一种有润肠、通便作用，第三种能解酸。他解释说，流

---

miserable *adj.* 可怜的

forehead *n.* 额；前额

capsule *n.* 胶囊

purgative *n.* 泻剂；泻药

he explained. He seemed to know all about influenza and said there was nothing to worry about if the fever did not go above one hundred and four ***degrees***. This was a light ***epidemic*** of flu and there was no danger if you avoided ***pneumonia***.

Back in the room I wrote the boy's temperature down and made a note of the time to give the ***various*** capsules.

"Do you want me to read to you?"

"All right. If you want to," said the boy. His face was very white and there were dark areas under his eyes. He lay still in the bed and seemed very detached from what was going on.

I read aloud from Howard Pyle's *Book* of Pirates; but I could see he was not following what I was reading.

感细菌只生存于酸性环境中。他好像对流感很有研究，还说，不烧到104度就不用担心。这是轻度流感，只要不引起肺炎就没有什么危险。

我回到房里记下孩子的体温，还记下了各种药物的服用时间。

“要不要给你念点什么听啊？”

“好吧，你要是想念就念吧，”孩子说。他的脸色十分苍白，眼窝下方有黑晕。躺在床上一动也不动，看上去对身边发生的一切都没有兴致。

我给他念霍华德·派尔的《海盗故事》，但看得出他并没有听。

---

degree *n.* （温度、压力等的）度

epidemic *n.* 流行病

pneumonia *n.* 肺炎

various *adj.* 各种各样的

"How do you feel, Schatz?" I asked him.

"Just the same, so far,"he said.

I sat at the foot of the bed and read to myself while I waited for it to be time to give another capsule. It would have been natural for him to go to sleep, but when I looked up he was looking at the foot of the bed, looking very ***strangely***.

"Why don't you try to sleep? I'll wake you up for the ***medicine***."

"I'd rather stay ***awake***."

After a while he said to me, "You don't have to stay in here with me, Papa, if it ***bothers*** you."

"It doesn't bother me."

"No, I mean you don't have to stay if it's going to bother you."

"你感觉怎么样，宝贝？"我问他。

"到目前为止，还是老样子，"他说。

我坐在床脚，干脆自顾自地读了起来，我得等着时间一到再给他服另一种药。按理说，他该睡过去了。但是，当我抬起头时，却看到他两眼盯着床脚，神情异常。

"你为什么不睡一会儿呢？到吃药时我会叫醒你的。"

"我宁愿醒着。"

过了一会，他对我说："你不必在这里陪我，爸爸，要是这事让你烦恼的话。"

"没有什么可烦恼的。"

"不，我是说要是这事将会给你带来烦恼的话，你就不必在这里陪我。"

---

strangely *adv.* 奇怪地

medicine *n.* 药；药剂

awake *adj.* 醒着的

bother *v.* 使烦恼

I thought perhaps he was a little ***lightheaded*** and after giving him the prescribed capsules at eleven o'clock I went out for a while.

It was a bright, cold day, the ground covered with a sleet that had frozen so that it seemed as if all the bare trees, the bushes, the cut brush and all the grass and the bare ground had been ***varnished*** with ice. I took the young Irish setter for a little walk up the road and along a frozen ***creek***, but it was difficult to stand or walk on the glassy surface and the red dog slipped and slithered and I fell twice, hard, once dropping my gun and having it slide away over the ice.

We flushed a covey of ***quail*** under a high clay bank with overhanging brush and I killed two as they went out of sight over

---

我想，他大概有些神志不清了。我按规定在11点时给他服了药。随后，便出去了一会儿。

那天天气很晴朗，也很寒冷，地面上覆盖的一层冻雨已经结成了冰。那光秃秃的落叶树木，那灌木丛，还有砍下的树枝，以及所有的草坪和空地都像涂了一层冰。我带着那条幼小的爱尔兰猎犬出去遛遛。我们走上公路，又沿着一条冰封的小溪往前走。但在那玻璃般光滑的冰面上，无论是站立还是行走，都是很困难的。红毛狗一路上连哧溜带滑，我自己也摔倒了两次，都挺实惠，其中一次连猎枪也甩掉了，在冰上滑出去老远。

高高的土堤上长着倒垂下来的灌木丛，我们从灌木丛下面轰起一群鹌

---

lightheaded *adj.* 眩晕的

varnish *v.* 给……上清漆

creek *n.* 小溪

quail *n.* 鹌鹑

the top of the bank. Some of the covey lit in trees, but most of them ***scattered*** into brush piles and it was necessary to jump on the ice-coated mounds of brush several times before they would flush. Coming out while you were poised unsteadily on the ***icy***, springy brush they made difficult shooting and I killed two, missed five, and started back pleased to have found a covey close to the house and happy there were so many left to find another day.

At the house they said the boy had ***refused*** to let anyone come into the room.

"You can't come in," he said. "You mustn't get what I have."

I went up to him and found him in exactly the ***position*** I had left

---

鹑。就在它们快要越过堤岸飞离视野时我击落了两只。有几只鹌鹑落在了树上，但大部分飞散了，钻进了灌木丛。它们得在裹了一层冰的树冠上跳上几跳，才能起飞。你在这些又滑又颤的树丛上摇摇晃晃尚未立稳，它们却飞了出来，使你很难瞄准。但我还是击落了两只，另有五只没有击中。动身返回时，我心情很愉快，因为在离家不远的地方发现了一群鹌鹑，猎获了两只，还剩下许多，改日可再来猎取。

回到家里后听说孩子不让任何人进入他的房间。

"你们不能进来，"他说。"你们绝不能染上我这种病。"

我来到他身边，发现他还像我离开时那样躺着，脸色苍白，但脸颊上

---

scatter *v.* 散开　　icy *adj.* 冰冷的
refuse *v.* 拒绝　　position *n.* 位置；方位

him, white-faced, but with the tops of his cheeks flushed by the fever, ***staring*** still, as he had stared, at the foot of the bed.

I took his ***temperature***.

"What is it?"

"Something like a hundred," I said. It was one hundred and two and four tenths.

"It was a hundred and two," he said.

"Who said so?"

"The doctor."

"Your temperature is all right," I said. "It's nothing to worry about."

烧出了两朵红晕，眼睛依旧一动不动地盯着床脚。

我给他量了体温。

"多少度？"

"大约100度，"我说。实际上是102.4度。

"原先是102度，"他说。

"谁说的？"

"医生。"

"你的体温没什么问题，"我说，"根本用不着担心。"

---

stare *v.* 凝视

temperature *n.* 温度

"I don't worry," he said, "but I can't keep from thinking."

"Don't think," I said. "Just take it easy."

"I'm taking it easy," he said and looked straight ahead. He was ***evidently*** holding tight onto himself about something.

"Take this with water."

"Do you think it will do any good?"

"Of course it will."

I sat down and opened the *Book of Pirate* and ***commenced*** to read, but I could see he was not following, so I stopped.

"About what time do you think I'm going to die?" he asked.

"What?"

"我倒不担心，"他说，"可我就是不能不想。"

"不要想了，"我说。"放心好了。"

"我倒没有什么不放心的，"他说着，眼睛直盯着前方。显然，他有什么心事，但却极力克制着不说。

"把这个用水吞下去。"

"你觉得有用吗？"

"当然有用。"

我坐下来，又打开了《海盗故事》，开始念给他听。但看得出他不在听，于是，我就不念了。

"你认为我得什么时候死呢？"他问道。

"你说什么？"

---

evidently *adv.* 显然；明显地　　**commence** *v.* 开始

"About how long will it be before I die?"

"You aren't going to die. What's the matter with you?"

"Oh, yes, I am. I heard him say a hundred and two."

"People don't die with a ***fever*** of one hundred and two. That's a silly way to talk."

"I know they do. At school in France the boys told me you can't live with forty-four degrees. I've got a hundred and two."

He had been waiting to die ***all day***, ever since nine o'clock in the morning.

"你看我还能活多久？"

"你不会死的。你怎么啦？"

"哦，我会死的。我听见他说102度了。"

"人烧到102度是不会死的。你这是在说傻话呢。"

"会的。在法国上学的时候，我就听说，烧到44度就不能活了。我已经到102度了。"

原来从上午9点钟起，他一整天都在等死啊。

---

fever *n.* 发烧

all day 整天

"You poor Schatz," I said. "It's like miles and ***kilometers***. You know, like how many kilometers we make when we do seventy miles in the car?"

"Oh," he said.

But his ***gaze*** at the foot of the bed relaxed slowly. The hold over himself relaxed too, finally, and the next day it was very ***slack*** and he cried very easily at little things that were of no ***importance***.

"这可怜的宝贝，"我说，"这就像英里和公里的区别一样。知道吗？就像我们开车开了70英里能折合成多少公里一样。"

"噢，"他说。

他那凝视床脚的目光渐渐放松了，心里的紧张状态也终于缓解了。第二天，他一点儿也打不起精神来，这还不说，为了一点点小事他还动不动就哭鼻子。

---

kilometer *n.* 公里；千米

gaze *n.* 盯；凝视

slack *adj.* 松弛的

importance *n.* 重要性；重大

10

A White Heron

Adapted from the story by Sarah Orne Jewett

Sarah Orne Jewett was born in 1849 in South Berwick, Maine. She lived there quietly near the sea most of her life. Her father was a doctor. As a child, she went with him on his ***trips*** to see sick people in Maine's fishing and farm ***villages***. She learned more this way than she learned at school, which she didn't like. She also learned by reading the many books in her parents' house.

白色的苍鹭

根据莎拉·奥恩·朱厄特的同名故事改写

莎拉·奥恩·朱厄特1849年生于缅因州的南贝里克。她一生中绝大部分时光都是在海边平静地度过。父亲是位医生。儿时，她就随父亲在缅因州的渔村和农场为病人巡诊。她以这种方式学到的东西超出了在学校里学到的东西，因为她不喜欢学校。她还通过阅读父母房间里的许多书籍来增长知识。年纪很小时，她就开始写故事。她所有的故事都

trip *n.* 旅行　　village *n.* 村庄

A WHITE HERON

She began writing stories when she was very young. All her stories were about the ***simple*** lives of the country people she had met on her trips with her father. Her stories show her love of nature as well as human nature. The woods, fields, and animals of Maine are almost like ***characters*** in her stories. Her best-known book is called *Country of the Pointed Firs*. (Maine is well known for its pine and fir trees-evergreens, as they are called.) In 1909, Sarah Orne Jewett died in the same house in which she had been born and raised.

I

The woods were already filled with ***shadows*** one June evening just before eight o'clock. Sylvia was driving her ***cow*** home. They turned deep into the dark woods. Their feet knew the way. The birds

---

是描写乡下人的简朴生活，这些人都是在随父巡诊时遇到的。故事表明她对大自然和人性的热爱。缅因州的森林、田野和动物与故事中的角色非常接近。她最著名的作品是《有刺杉的乡村》（缅因州以松树和杉树而闻名，这些树木也叫常青树）。1909年，莎拉·奥恩·朱厄特死在生养她的那所房子里。

I

在一个夏日的黄昏，还没到八点，森林里就已经阴暗下来。西尔维亚正赶着牛儿回家。她和牛儿一步步走进了幽暗的林中。她们靠脚步的摸索，找到回家的路。鸟儿在头顶的树枝上啁啾，好像在悄悄地互道晚安。

---

simple *adj.* 简单的；朴素的
character *n.* 角色；特征
shadow *n.* 阴影；影子
cow *n.* 奶牛；母牛

in the trees above her head seemed to sing "good night" to each other quietly. The air was soft and sweet. Sylvia felt a part of the ***gray*** shadows and the moving leaves. To Sylvia, it seemed ***as if*** she hadn't really been alive before she came to live with her grandmother in this beautiful place.

Suddenly she heard a call. Not a bird's call, which would have had a friendly sound. It was a young man's call, sudden and loud. Sylvia left the cow alone and hid behind some ***leaves***. But the young man saw her.

"Halloa, little girl. How far is it to the road?"

Sylvia was afraid. She answered in a soft voice, "A good ways..."

林间的空气柔和而又芬芳。西尔维亚感受着那些灰暗的阴影和婆娑的枝叶。她觉得来到这个美丽的地方与奶奶一同生活之前，好像从未真正体验过生活。

突然，她听到一种喊叫声。那肯定不是鸟儿发出的叫声，鸟儿的叫声听起来是很友善的。那是一个青年男子的喊声，声音短促而洪亮。西尔维亚丢下母牛躲到树后，但那青年还是看见她了。

"喂，小姑娘。从这儿到公路还有多远？"

西尔维亚很紧张。她轻声回答说："还有很远……"

---

gray *adj.* 灰色的

as if 好像

suddenly *adv.* 突然地

leaf *n.* 树叶

"I'm ***hunting*** for some birds," the young man said kindly. He carried a gun over his ***shoulder***. "I am lost and need a friend very much. Don't be afraid. Speak up, and tell me what your name is. Do you think I can spend the night at your house and go out hunting in the morning?"

Sylvia was more afraid than ever. But she said her name, and ***dropped*** her head like a broken flower.

Her grandmother was waiting at the door. The cow gave a "moo" as the three arrived.

"Yes, you should speak for yourself, you old cow," said her grandmother. "Where was she hiding so long, Sylvy?"

"我在猎鸟，"青年友好地说，肩上扛着一支猎枪。"迷路了，非常需要一个朋友的帮助。不要害怕，开口说话吧，告诉我你叫什么名字。你看我可不可以在你们家过夜，明天早晨再出来打猎？"

西尔维亚更紧张了。但她还是说出了自己的名字，一说完马上就像一朵被折断了的花一样把头低下。

奶奶正在门口等她。等他们到达的时候，那牛儿"哞"地叫了一声。

"是啊，你真应该自己说说，你这头老牛，"奶奶说。"她在哪儿躲了这么久，西尔维？"

---

hunt *v.* 狩猎

shoulder *n.* 肩；肩膀

drop *v.* 使落下；垂下

Sylvia didn't speak. She thought her grandmother should be afraid of the ***stranger***.

But the young man stood his gun beside the door. He dropped a heavy gun-bag beside it. He said good evening and told the old woman his story.

"Dear me, yes," she answered. "You might do better if you went out to the road a mile away. But you're welcome to what we've got. I'll milk the cow ***right away***. Now, you make yourself at home. Sylvy, ***step*** round, and set a plate for the ***gentleman***!"

Sylvia stepped. She was glad to have something to do, and she was hungry.

西尔维亚没有说话。她觉得奶奶见了这个陌生人会感到害怕。

但青年把猎枪放在门旁，把沉重的枪套也扔在旁边，对奶奶道一声晚安后就开始给奶奶讲起自己到这儿来的缘由。

"哎呀，可真是的，"她回答说。"你要是再走一英里上了公路就好了。不过，既然来了，那就欢迎了。我这就挤奶去。你请便吧。西尔维，转转身，活动两步，给这位先生摆个盘子！"

西尔维亚去摆盘子了。她很高兴能有点事情可做，再说，她也饿了。

---

stranger *n.* 陌生人

step *v.* 走；迈步

right away 立刻

gentleman *n.* 先生；绅士

The young man was surprised to find such a ***comfortable***, clean house in the deep woods of Maine. He thought this was the best supper he had eaten in a month. After ***supper*** the new-made friends sat in the shadowed ***doorway*** to watch the moon come up. The young man listened happily to the grandmother's stories. The old woman talked most about her children. About her daughter, Sylvia's mother, who had a hard life with so many children. About her son, Dan, who left home for California many years ago.

"Sylvy is like Dan," she said happily. "She knows every foot of the woods. She plays with the woods animals and ***feeds*** the birds. Yes, she'd give her own meals to them, if I didn't watch her!"

那青年看到在缅因州的密林深处能有这样一户既舒适又干净的人家感到非常意外。他觉得这是一个月来吃过的最好的一顿晚饭。饭后，这三位新交的朋友坐在门口的阴凉处看着明月慢慢升起。那青年愉快地听着老奶奶讲故事。老人讲了很多有关自己子女的事，讲了她的女儿，也就是西尔维亚的母亲。她生了很多孩子，日子过得艰难。还讲了她儿子，名字叫“丹”，很多年前就离家去了加利福尼亚。

“西尔维很像丹，”她高兴地说。“对森林知道得一清二楚，跟林中的动物玩耍，给林中的鸟儿喂食。是啊，我要是不看着她，她连自己吃的饭菜都想给鸟儿吃呢！”

---

comfortable *adj.* 舒适的
doorway *n.* 门口
supper *n.* 晚餐
feed *v.* 喂养

"So Sylvy knows all about birds, does she?" asked the young man. "I am trying to catch one of every kind."

"Do you keep them ***alive***?" asked the old woman.

"No. I stuff them in order to save them," he answered. "I have almost a hundred of them. And I caught every one myself."

Sylvia was watching a ***toad*** jump in the moonlight.

"I followed a bird here that I want to catch. A white ***heron***. You would know a heron if you saw it, Sylvy," he said, ***hopefully***. "A strange, tall white bird with long, thin legs."

Sylvia's heart stopped. She knew that strange white bird.

"这么说，西尔维知道所有的鸟儿，是吗？"年轻人问道。"每一种鸟我都想捕获一只。"

"你是养着它们吗？"老太太问。

"不，我给它们填充起来，制成标本，为的是挽救它们，"他回答说。"我差不多已经有一百种了。而且每一种都是我自己抓到的。"

塞尔维亚正在观察一只癞蛤蟆在月光下跳跃。

"我正是因为追踪一只鸟儿才来到这里的，那是一只白色的苍鹭。你要是见过苍鹭，就会知道的，西尔维，"他满怀希望地说。"那是一种奇怪的，高大的白鸟，有着两条长长的细腿。"

西尔维亚的心都停止了跳动。她知道那只奇怪的白鸟。

---

alive *adj.* 活着的
toad *n.* 蟾蜍；癞蛤蟆
heron *n.* 鹭；苍鹭
hopefully *adv.* 抱有希望地

"I want that bird more than anything," the young man went on. "I would give ten dollars to know where its nest is."

Sylvia couldn't ***believe*** there was so much money in the world. But she watched the toad and said nothing.

The next day Sylvia went with the young man into the woods. He was kind and ***friendly***, and told her many things about the birds. She wasn't afraid of him anymore. Perhaps in her heart a dream of love was born. But she couldn't understand why he killed and ***stuffed*** the birds he liked so much.

"我比什么都渴望那只白鸟，"青年接着说。"谁能告诉我鸟巢在哪儿，我就付给他十美元。"

西尔维亚简直不敢相信世界上居然会有那么多钱。但她只是默默地看着那只癞蛤蟆，什么也没说。

第二天，西尔维亚跟着青年走进森林。他很友善，给她讲了很多有关鸟的事。她不再怕他了。在她心中或许还有一种朦胧的爱在悄然升起。但她不能理解他为什么要把自己那么喜欢的鸟儿杀死并填充起来。

---

believe *v.* 相信
friendly *adj.* 友好的
stuff *v.* 塞满；填塞

II

At the *edge* of the woods a great *pine* tree stood. Sylvia knew it well. That night she thought of the tree. If she climbed it early in the morning, she could see the whole world. Couldn't she watch the heron fly, and find its hidden nest? What an *adventure* it would be! And how happy her friend would be! The young man and the old woman slept well that night, but Sylvia thought of her adventure. She forgot to think of sleep. At last, when the night birds stopped singing, she quietly left the house.

There was the tall pine tree, still asleep in the moonlight. First she climbed a smaller tree *next to* it. Then she made the dangerous step across to the old pine. The birds in the woods below her were

---

II

在森林边缘，有一棵高大的松树。西尔维亚对它非常熟悉。那天晚上，她想到了那棵树。如果在清晨爬上树去，就能看到整个世界。难道她看不到那只苍鹭起飞，看不到它那隐蔽的鸟巢吗？那是一种怎样的冒险啊！而她的朋友将会多么高兴啊！那天晚上，青年和老奶奶睡得很熟，但西尔维亚考虑起自己的冒险，竟忘记了睡眠。最后，当夜莺停止歌唱时，她悄悄地起身走了出去。

正是那棵高大的松树，在月光下安然地熟睡着。她先爬上了旁边一棵较为低矮的树。然后冒着危险从这棵树上跨到了那棵老松树上。森林中

---

edge *n.* 边缘

pine *n.* 松树

adventure *n.* 冒险

next to 紧挨着

waking up. She must climb faster if she wanted to see the heron as it left its nest. The tree seemed to grow taller as she went up. The pine tree must have been surprised to feel this small person climbing up. It must have loved this new animal in its arms. Perhaps it moved its branches a little, to help her climb. Sylvia's face ***shone*** like a star when she reached the top. She was tired, but very happy. She could see ships out to sea. Woods and farms lay for miles and miles around her. The birds sang louder and louder. At last the sun came up. Where was the heron's ***nest***? Look, look, Sylvia! A white spot rises up from the green trees below. The ***spot*** grows larger. The heron flies close. A wild, light bird, wide wings, and a long thin neck. He stops in the tree beyond Sylvia. Wait, wait, Sylvia! Do not move a

---

她脚下的鸟儿纷纷醒来。她必须加快速度往上爬，否则，在那苍鹭离巢起飞时就看不见它了。她越是往上爬，那松树好像也越是在长高。它一定是很吃惊地感觉到这个小人儿正在往上爬。它一定是非常喜欢这个新动物在怀里爬的感觉。也许，它还轻轻地动一动枝条来助她一臂之力。西尔维亚爬到顶部时，兴奋得脸像天上的星星一样闪着明亮的光辉。她筋疲力尽，但同时也异常兴奋。她能够远眺大海里的各种船只。周围数英里绵延不绝的森林和农场也尽收眼底。鸟儿的啁啾声一阵比一阵高亢。最后，太阳升起来了。苍鹭的巢在哪儿？瞧，瞧，西尔维亚！一个白色的小点从下边的绿树上升起。白点越来越大。苍鹭飞近了。一只野性的、明亮的鸟儿，有着宽阔的羽翼和修长的细颈，停在西尔维亚旁边的那棵树上了。别动，

---

shine *v.* 发光；照耀

nest *n.* 巢；窝

spot *n.* 斑点

foot or a ***finger***, to frighten it away!

A moment later, Sylvia ***sighs***. A large company of noisy birds comes to the tree, and the heron goes away. It flies down to its home in the green world below. Sylvia knows its secret now. She climbs back down. Now she is almost crying. Her fingers hurt, and her feet slip. She ***wonders*** what the young man will say to her. What will he think when she tells him how to find the heron's nest?

"Sylvy, Sylvy," her grandmother called, but nobody answered.

The young man woke up and dressed. He wanted to begin hunting again. He was sure Sylvia knew something about the white heron. Here she comes now. Her small face is white, her old dress is ***torn*** and dirty. The grandmother and the young man wait at the door

---

别动，西尔维亚！千万不要动，哪怕只是轻微地动一动手脚也绝对不行。千万不要把它惊飞了！

过了一会儿，西尔维亚叹了一口气。一大群聒噪的鸟儿飞过来，落在这棵树上，苍鹭飞走了。向下飞去，向下面绿色世界里自己的家飞去。西尔维亚现在知道了它的秘密。她从树上往下爬，手磨破了，还失足跌落下来。她不知道那青年会对她说什么。如果她把发现鸟巢的事告诉他的话，他会怎么想呢?

“西尔维，西尔维！”奶奶在叫她，但是没有人回应。

那青年醒来，穿好衣服，又要开始打猎了。他相信西尔维亚肯定知道一些有关白色苍鹭的情况。这不，她回来了。小脸煞白，旧衣服又脏又破。老奶奶和青年等在门口有话要问她。到了该说出鸟巢的时候了。

---

finger *n.* 手指

sigh *v.* 叹气

wonder *v.* 想知道

tear *v.* 扯裂；撕开

to question her. The time has come to tell about the heron's nest.

But Sylvia does not speak. The young man looks into her eyes. He will make them rich. She wants to make him happy. He waits to hear the story she can tell.

No, she must *keep silent*! What is it that keeps her quiet? This is the first time the world has put out a hand to her. Does she have to push it away *because of* a bird? She hears again the wind blowing in the pine tree. She remembers how the white heron flew through the *golden* air. She remembers how they watched the sea and the morning together. Sylvia cannot speak. She cannot tell the heron's *secret* and give its life away.

但西尔维亚并不说。青年仔细琢磨她的眼神。他会使她们富有；她也想让他高兴。他在等着她把该说的说给他听。

不，她必须保持沉默！是什么使她保持沉默呢？这是这个世界第一次向她伸出手来。难道就因为一只鸟儿她就得把它推开吗？她听到风儿在松树间吹拂。她记得那白色的苍鹭在金色的晨曦中飞翔的情景，记得她是怎样同苍鹭一起观看大海和黎明。西尔维亚说不出话来。她无法说出苍鹭的秘密，她不能背叛它。

---

keep silent 保持沉默

golden *adj.* 金色的

because of 因为

secret *n.* 秘密

Poor Sylvia! She was sad when the young man went away. She could have helped him. She would have ***followed*** him like a dog. She would have loved him as a dog loves! Many nights ***afterwards*** Sylvia remembered his "Halloa" as she came home with the cow. She forgot the ***sharp*** sound of his gun. She forgot the birds, wet with blood. Were the birds better friends than the hunter? Who can tell?

Oh, Woods! Oh, ***Summertime***! Remember what riches were lost to her. Bring her your riches instead, your beauties and your gifts. Tell all your secrets to this lonely country child!

可怜的西尔维亚！当青年离去的时候，她感到很悲伤。她原本可以帮助他的。原本可以像一只狗一样跟在他后面，像一只狗那样忠诚地爱他啊！此后的许多夜晚，西尔维亚赶着牛儿回家的时候都能想起他的那句“喂”来。然而，她会忘记他那尖利的枪声，会忘记曾经见过的那些血淋淋的鸟类，鸟儿比起猎人来倒是更好的朋友吗？谁知道呢？

噢，森林！噢，夏天！请你们记着她失去了多么宝贵的东西。那么，就请把你们的财富，你们的美和你们的礼物送给她吧。把你们所有的秘密都告诉给这位孤独的乡村孩子吧！

---

follow *v.* 跟随

afterwards *adv.* 以后；后来

sharp *adj.* 尖锐的；刺耳的

summertime *n.* 夏季

The Ingrate

Adapted from the story by Paul Laurence Dunbar

Paul Laurence Dunbar was born in Dayton, Ohio, in 1872. His father had been a slave; he had been owned by a white man in the South. Like Josh, one of the two main characters in "*The Ingrate*," Dunbar's father ***escaped*** to freedom in the North and fought for the North in the Civil War (1861—1865). Dunbar was ***sickly*** as a child and spent much of his time alone reading. He began to write as a young man, and at first he published mostly ***poetry***. He earned very little money from his writing, and he was working as an elevator operator when he met the well-known writer and editor William Dean

忘恩负义

根据保罗·劳伦斯·邓巴的同名故事改写

保罗·劳伦斯·邓巴1872年生于俄亥俄州代顿市。其父有过和《忘恩负义》中两个主人公之一乔希类似的经历：曾为黑奴，曾受雇于南方的黑人。为了自由逃往北方，之后又参加了南北战争（1861—1865）。小时候体弱多病的邓巴独自利用大量的时间进行阅读。邓巴年轻时就开始写作，起初发表的作品多为诗歌。他写作赚的钱很少，当他遇见著名作家兼编辑威廉·迪安·豪威尔斯时他是一名电梯工。威廉·迪安·豪威尔斯对邓巴很感兴趣，曾为邓巴的诗集《下层人生的诗

escape *v.* 逃跑；逃走　　sickly *adj.* 常生病的；爱闹病的

poetry *n.* 诗；诗歌

Howells. He took an interest in Dunbar and wrote an introduction to a collection of Dunbar's poetry, *Lyrics of Lowly Life*. This and his later books of poetry made Dunbar well known as a poet during his lifetime. Now, his novels and stories are better known than his poetry. Dunbar died in Dayton in 1906, at the age of only thirty-four.

I

Mr. Leckler was a man of high ***principle***. He had often said this to Mrs. Leckler. She was often called in to listen to him. Mr. Leckler was one of those people with an ***endless*** hunger for advice, though he never acted on it. Mrs. Leckler knew this, but like a good little wife, she always offered him her little gifts of ***advice***. Today, her husband's mind was troubled—as usual, troubled about a question of principle.

"Mrs. Leckler," he said, "I am troubled in my mind. I'm troubled

---

歌》作序。这部和此后的诗集使他在一生中作为诗人而广为人知。如今邓巴的小说和故事比其诗歌更为知名。邓巴卒于1906年，年仅34岁。

I

莱柯勒先生是一位非常讲究原则的人，他经常对莱柯勒夫人这么说。他夫人三天两头就得被他叫进去听他说上一通。莱柯勒先生属于这样一种人：总是没完没了地渴望得到别人的忠告，尽管从不付诸实施。莱柯勒夫人对此心知肚明，不过作为一位娇小的妻子，她总是不吝于给他一点儿，全当是送给他一件小小的礼物。今天她丈夫又心烦意乱了——和往常一样，还是因为一个原则问题。

"莱柯勒夫人，"他说："我心烦意乱，老是为一个原则问题而困

---

principle *n.* 原理；原则

endless *adj.* 无止境的；无穷尽的

advice *n.* 忠告

by a question of principle."

"Yes, Mr. Leckler?" his wife asked.

"If I were a cheating northern ***Yankee***, I would be rich now. But I am too ***honest*** and generous. I always let my principles get between me and my duty." Mr. Leckler was sure of his own ***goodness***. "Now, here is the question that troubles my principles. My slave, Josh, has been working for Mr. Eckley in Lexington. I think that city cheat has been dishonest. He lied about how many hours Josh worked, and ***cut down*** his pay for it. Now, of course, I don't care, the question of a dollar or two is nothing to me. But it's a different question for poor Josh." Mr. Leckler's voice became sadder. "You know, Josh wants to buy his freedom from me. And I generously give him part of what he earns. Every dollar Mr. Eckley cheats him of cuts down his pay and

---

扰。"

"怎么回事儿，莱柯勒先生？"妻子问。

"假如我是个不诚实的北佬，现在早就发财了。但是我太诚实、太慷慨了，做什么事都要首先考虑是不是违背原则。"莱柯勒先生对自己的仁慈深信不疑。"现在就有一个关乎原则的问题。我的奴隶，乔希，这些天来一直在列克星敦给艾克雷先生干活。那个城里人，我看是个骗子。他少报乔希的工时，克扣工钱。当然，我到不在乎这个，一两块钱对我来说也不算什么。可是，对可怜的乔希就不一样了。"莱柯勒先生的语调越发悲伤起来，他说："你知道，乔希想从我这儿赎回自由。我倒是很慷慨地从他赚的钱里拿出一部分给他。可艾克雷呢？他从他那骗走的每一块钱都是

Yankee *n.* 美国佬；美国人
honest *adj.* 诚实的；老实的
goodness *n.* 善良
cut down 减少；削减

puts farther away his hopes of freedom."

Mrs. Leckler knew that Mr. Leckler let Josh keep only one-tenth of what he earned for ***extra*** work. So Mr. Eckley's ***dishonesty*** hurt her husband more than it hurt Josh. But she didn't say anything about that. She only asked, "But what troubles you about duty and principle here, Mr. Leckler?"

Mr. Leckler answered, "Well, if Josh knew how to read and write and do numbers..."

"Mr. Leckler, are you ***crazy***!" she cried.

"Listen to me, my dear, and give me your advice. This is an important question. If Josh knew these things he wouldn't be ***cheated*** when he worked away from me."

在减少他的所得，这就等于是逼他一步一步远离所渴望的自由啊。"

莱柯勒夫人知道，乔希额外干活赚的钱莱柯勒先生只给他十分之一，所以艾克雷先生的欺骗实际上是让她丈夫蒙受更大的损失。但她什么也没说，只是问："可是，莱柯勒先生，就责任和原则来说，这又有什么可让你烦恼的呢？"

莱柯勒先生答道："嗯，要是乔希能写会算就好了……"

"你疯了吗，莱柯勒先生！"她脱口喊道。

"听我说，亲爱的，然后你再跟我说说你是怎么想的。这件事很重要。要是乔希有这些本事的话，那他离开我到外面去干活就不会受骗了。"

---

extra *adj.* 额外的　　dishonesty *n.* 不诚实

crazy *adj.* 疯狂的　　cheat *v.* 欺骗

"But teaching a slave..."

"Yes, Mrs. Leckler, that's what troubles me. I know my duty—I know what the law and other people say about teaching a slave. But it is against my principles that that poor black man is being cheated. Really, Mrs. Leckler, I think I may teach him secretly, so he can ***defend*** himself."

"Well, of course," said Mrs. Leckler, "do what you think is best."

"I knew you would agree with me," he answered. "I'm glad to have your advice, my dear." And so this master of principle walked out to see his ***valuable*** slave. He was very ***pleased*** with his generosity. "I'll get Eckley next time!" he said to himself.

Josh, the subject of Mr. Leckler's principles, worked as a ***plasterer***

"但是教一个奴隶……"

"是啊，莱柯勒夫人，我不正为这事心烦嘛。我知道我的责任——我懂法律，也知道要教一个奴隶读书写字别人会怎么说。可是，眼睁睁看着一个可怜的黑人受骗而无动于衷，那不是违背我做事的原则吗？真的，莱柯勒夫人，我觉得可以偷偷地教他，这样，他以后就有能力自卫了。"

"哦，当然了，"莱柯勒夫人说："你觉得怎么做好就怎么做好了。"

"我就知道你会同意的，"他说。"很高兴得到你的忠告，亲爱的。"说完这些，这位原则大师就出去找那他个颇有价值的奴隶去了。他对自己的慷慨大度非常满意，自言自语道："下次我要让艾克雷吃不消！"

乔希，这个涉及莱柯勒先生的原则问题的中心人物在莱柯勒先生的

---

defend *v.* 保卫；守卫
valuable *adj.* 值钱的；有价值的
pleased *adj.* 满意的
plasterer *n.* 粉刷匠；泥水匠

on Mr. Leckler's ***plantation***, working on the walls and ceilings of the plantation's many buildings. Josh was very good at his work, and other men wanted him to work for them, too. So Mr. Leckler made money by letting Josh work on their plantations in his free time. Josh was a man of high ***intelligence***. When he asked Mr. Leckler if he could buy his freedom with the money he made on other plantations, Mr. Leckler quickly agreed. He knew he could let his valuable slave keep only a little of the money he earned. Most of what Josh earned would ***belong to*** his ***master***. Of course, Mr. Leckler knew that when the black man learned his numbers things would change. But it would be years before Josh could earn $2,000, the price Mr. Leckler asked for Josh's freedom. And, Mr. Leckler thought, by the time Josh came

---

种植园里当泥水匠，给种植园中许多建筑砌墙，建天花板。乔希的活干得特别好，很多别的园主也想要他去干活。所以，莱柯勒先生就让乔希在闲暇时到那些种植园去干活，靠这个来赚钱。乔希是个智商很高的人。他问莱柯勒先生他是否可以到别的种植园去干活，用赚来的钱赎回自由，莱柯勒先生一听立马表示同意。他知道这个能干的奴隶从中得到的只是一小部分，赚来的大头儿可都是这个奴隶主的。当然，莱柯勒先生也知道这个黑奴要是学会了算术的话，情况就会有所变化，但是，乔希要想攒够两千美金（那是莱柯勒对乔希赎回自由的要价）得是好多年以后的事了。莱柯勒先生

---

plantation *n.* 种植园
intelligence *n.* 智力；智慧
belong to 属于
master *n.* 主人；雇主

close to earning the money, the cost of a slave's freedom might suddenly go higher.

When Josh heard his master's plan, his eyes shone with pleasure, and he worked even harder than before. Even Mr. Leckler, who knew his plasterer's intelligence, was surprised how quickly Josh was learning to read, write, and ***figure***. Mr. Leckler didn't know that on one of Josh's work trips a ***freed*** slave had given Josh some lessons. Josh already knew the beginnings of how to read before he began his lessons with Mr. Leckler. But he certainly wasn't going to tell Mr. Leckler that.

So a year passed away, and Mr. Leckler thought Josh had learned enough.

盘算着，就算真的到了差不多攒够的时候，赎金没准儿还会突然上涨呢。

乔希听到主人的计划，两眼顿时放出喜悦的光芒，干起活儿来更卖力了。莱柯勒先生虽然知道乔希很聪明，但却没有料到乔希居然能这么快就学会读、写、算。他哪里知道，一次外出干活时，乔希已经跟一个赎了身的奴隶学了一些。也就是说，在莱柯勒先生教他之前就已经有了一点基础，只是没打算把这事告诉莱柯勒先生。

一年之后，莱柯勒先生觉得乔希学得差不多了。

---

figure *v.* 计算

free *v.* 释放；解放

"You know, Josh," he said, "I have already gone against my principles and *disobeyed* the law for you. A man can't *go against* his principles too far, even for someone who is being cheated. I think you can *take care of* yourself now."

"Oh, yes, sir, I guess I can," said Josh.

"And you shouldn't be seen with any books, now."

"Oh, no, sir, certainly not," Josh said *obediently*. He certainly didn't plan to be seen with any books.

Just now, Mr. Leckler saw the good in what he had done. His heart was full of a great joy. Mr. Eckley was building on to his house, and asked Josh to do the plastering. When the job was done, Josh

---

"你知道，乔希，"他说，"为了你，我可是违背了自己的原则，也违背了法律。违背原则的事不能做得过分，即便是为了帮助一个受骗的人。我想，你现在可以照顾好自己了。"

"嗯，主人，我也觉得我能行。"乔希说。

"你可不能让人看见你随身带着书本什么的。"

"哦，不会，主人，我当然不会，"乔希顺从地说。他当然不想让人看到他有书。

眼下，莱柯勒先生终于看到了自己种下的"善果"，满心欢喜。艾克雷先生当时正在扩建房宅，他让乔希过去当泥水匠。工程结束后，乔希

---

disobey *v.* 违反

take care of 照顾

go against 违反；反对

obediently *adv.* 顺从地

figured that Eckley had cheated him again. Eckley was very ***surprised*** when the black man looked at the numbers and showed him his dishonesty, but he passed him the two dollars. "Leckler did this," Mr. Eckley thought to himself. "Teaching a black his numbers! Leckler just wanted more money for himself! I should call the law!"

Mr. Leckler was very pleased when he heard that Josh had caught Eckley cheating. He said to himself, "Ha! I caught him, the old thief!" But to Mrs. Leckler he said, "You see, my dear, my ***craziness*** in teaching Josh was right. See how much money he saved for himself."

"What did he save?" asked the little wife without thinking.

通过计算得知艾克雷又一次骗了他。当这黑人看着账目戳穿骗局时，艾克雷大吃一惊，不得不把克扣掉的两美元还给了乔希。“这一定是莱柯勒干的，”艾克雷心里琢磨着。“教一个黑奴算账！莱柯勒纯粹是想为自己多捞钱，我非告他不可！”

莱柯勒先生听说乔希当场戳穿艾克雷的骗局，非常高兴。他自言自语道：“这个惯偷儿，可把他给抓住了！”但是，他跟莱柯勒太太却说：“看到了吧，亲爱的。当时我教乔希识字，你还说我疯了，你看看乔希给自己挽回了多少损失！”

“挽回了多少什么？”这小妇人不假思索地问。

---

surprised *adj.* 感到惊讶的

craziness *n.* 愚蠢

Her husband turned red, and then answered, "Well, of course it was only 20 cents saved for him, but to a slave buying his freedom, every cent ***counts***. It is not the money, Mrs. Leckler, it's the principle of the thing."

"Yes," said the lady obediently.

II

It is easy enough for the master to order the body of a slave, "This far you may go, and no further." The master has laws and chains to hold the slave back. But what master can say to the mind of a slave, "I order you to stop learning"? Josh had begun to eat the ***forbidden*** fruit of learning, and he was hungry for more. Night after night he sat

---

她丈夫脸红了，接着回答道："哦，当然，对他来说，不过是二十美分而已。但是，对一个要赎身的奴隶来说，每一分钱都是大事！再说，这并不是钱的问题，莱柯勒夫人，这是事关原则的大事。"

"说得对，"他太太顺从地说。

II

借助于法律和锁链，奴隶主要想束缚一个奴隶的身体很容易——"你只准走这么远，多一点也不行。"但是要想束缚一个奴隶的心，他得说什么呢？说"我命令你停止学习"？乔希已经品尝过学文化这颗禁果，而且

---

count *v.* 有价值；有重要性

forbidden *adj.* 被禁止的

by his lonely fire and read one of his few books. Other slaves ***laughed at*** him. They told him to get a wife. But Josh had no time for love or ***marriage***. He had other hopes than to have his children be slaves to Mr. Leckler. To him, slavery was the dark night in which he dreamed of freedom. His dream was to own himself—to be the master of his own hands and feet, of his whole body. When he thought of this, something would catch at his heart, and breath came hard between his ***lips***. But he was quiet and ***obedient*** before his master, and Mr. Leckler was pleased. Usually intelligence in a slave meant trouble. But who seemed more untroubled than Josh? Mr. Leckler said to his wife, "You see, my dear, it's important to do the right thing, even to a black."

对此的渴望已经一发不可收拾。尽管他的书很有限，但夜复一夜，他独自坐在火边读着他那仅有的几本书。伙伴们嘲笑他，让他干脆娶个老婆算了。但是乔希没时间谈情说爱、娶妻生子。他有他的希望，决不想让自己的孩子接着给莱柯勒当奴隶。在他看来，奴隶制就是那漫漫的黑夜，在这漫漫的黑夜中他梦想着自由。他梦想拥有自己，做自己的主人。一想到这些，他就觉得有什么东西攫住了他的心，使他呼吸困难。但是，在主人面前，他仍然表现得平静、顺从，莱柯勒先生对此也很满意。一般说来，奴隶的智慧意味着奴隶主的麻烦。但是，有谁能像乔希那样从不惹是生非呢？莱柯勒先生对妻子说："看到了吧，亲爱的，做事要正直，即便是对

---

laugh at 嘲笑

lip *n.* 嘴唇

marriage *n.* 结婚

obedient *adj.* 顺从的

All this time, the white hills of the Yankee North seemed to call to Josh. The north wind told him that in the North he would be a slave *no longer*. Josh knew it would be hard to win his freedom. *Worst of all* was the law. It stood like a stone wall between *slavery* and freedom, between slavery and Josh's hopes. Then one day, when he was working away from home, a voice called to him from the *woods*, "Be brave!" And later that night the voice called to him like the north wind, "Follow."

"It seems to me that Josh should have come home tonight," said Mr. Leckler. "But maybe he got through too late to catch a train." In the morning he said, "Well, he's not here yet. He must have to do some extra work. If he doesn't get home tonight, I'll go up there."

黑人也不例外，这是很重要的。"

在这段时间里，北方那白雪覆盖的群山似乎一直在呼唤乔希。北风告诉他到了北方他将不再为奴。乔希知道要想赢得自由绝非易事。最大的障碍就是法律，它像一堵石墙挡在奴隶制和乔希的梦想之间。突然，有一天，就在他外出干活时，他听到树林中有个声音向他喊道："勇敢点！"那天晚上，那个声音就像北风一样再次呼唤他："一起走吧。"

"乔希好像应该今晚回来，"莱柯勒先生说。"也可能收工太晚了，没赶上火车。"到了早上，他又说："他怎么还没回来，一定是又加活儿了。要是他今晚还不回来，我就得去看看了。"

---

no longer 不再

slavery *n.* 奴隶制度

worst of all 最糟糕的是

woods *n.* 树林

That night he did take the train to where Josh had been working. He learned that Josh had left the night before. But where could he have gone? For the first time, Mr. Leckler *realized* that Josh had *run away*. Mr. Leckler was very angry. He knew that the most valuable slave on his plantation was going north to freedom. He walked the floor all night, but he couldn't go after Josh until morning.

Early the next day, he put the dogs on Josh's trail. The dogs followed it into the woods, but in a few minutes they came back, crying and lost. Josh had played an old slave *trick*—he had put hot *pepper* in his footprints. Finally the dogs found Josh's trail further in

---

到了晚上，他真就坐上火车去了乔希干活的地方，得知乔希前一天晚上就走了。但乔希能到哪儿去呢？莱柯勒先生这才第一次意识到乔希逃走了。他气得不行。他知道他的种植园里最能给他赚钱的奴隶逃到北方，寻求自由去了。整个晚上他都在屋子里走来走去，无计可施，因为在天亮之前他没法儿去追乔希。

第二天一大早，他带上几条猎狗去追踪乔希。狗群追进树林，可是，几分钟后又回来了，它们失去了线索，嗷嗷乱叫。原来，乔希用了奴隶逃亡时用的老把戏——在脚印里撒了辣椒粉。但猎狗最终还是在树林深处嗅到了乔希留下的气味儿。莱柯勒一直追踪到六英里外的一个火车站。莱柯

---

realize *v.* 认清；认识到

run away 逃跑

trick *n.* 诡计；恶作剧

pepper *n.* 胡椒粉

the woods. Leckler followed the trail until he came to a train station about six miles away. Mr. Leckler asked the ***stationmaster*** if he had seen a black get on the train.

"Yes," the man said, "two nights ago."

"But why did you let him go without a ***pass***?" cried Mr. Leckler in anger.

"I didn't," said the stationmaster. "He had a written pass ***signed*** 'James Leckler.'"

"Lies, lies!" cried Mr. Leckler. "He wrote it himself!"

"Well, how could I know?" answered the stationmaster. "Our blacks around here don't know how to write."

Mr. Leckler suddenly decided to keep quiet. Josh was probably

---

勒先生问站长看没看到一个黑人乘坐火车。

"看到过，"站长说，"那是两天前的事了。"

"可是，没有通行证你怎么能让他上车呢？"莱柯勒先生喊道。

"我当然不会，"站长说："可他有通行证啊，上面签着'詹姆斯·莱柯勒'的名字。"

"撒谎！撒谎！"莱柯勒先生叫喊着。"那是他自己写上去的！"

"哼，我怎么会知道？"站长答道。"这一带的黑人都不会写字。"

莱柯勒先生突然决定不再跟他废话。乔希这会儿可能已经到了那些主张废奴的北佬的怀抱里了。除了登广告要乔希回来以外，别无他法。他回

---

stationmaster *n.* （火车站）站长 pass *n.* 通行证

sign *v.* 签上；署上

in the arms of some Yankee ***abolitionist*** by now. There was nothing to do but put up ***advertisements*** for Josh's return. He went home and spoke angrily to his wife.

"You see, Mrs. Leckler, this is what comes of my ***generous*** heart. I taught a black to read and write. Now look how he uses this knowledge. Oh, the ingrate, the ***ingrate***! He turns against me the weapon I gave him to defend himself! Here's the most valuable slave on my plantation gone—gone, I tell you—and all because of my kindness. It isn't his value I'm thinking about. It's the principle of the thing—the ingratitude he has shown me. Oh, if I ever catch him—hum!"

Just at this time, Josh was six miles north of the Ohio River. A kind Quaker was saying softly to Josh, "Lie quiet. You will be safe

---

到家里，怒气冲冲地对老婆说：

"你瞧，莱柯勒夫人，我的宽宏大度换来的就是这个。我把一个黑人教得能写会算，到头来怎么样？看看他是怎么利用他学到的知识来对付我的吧。唉，忘恩负义啊，真是忘恩负义！他居然用我教给他的自卫办法来对付我了！这可是我园里最值钱的奴隶啊，他跑了，跑了！我告诉你，都是因为我太仁慈了！我倒不是在乎他的所谓价值，我在乎的是这件事的原则——他对我忘恩负义。哼，我要是抓到他——哼！"

此时此刻，乔希已经到了俄亥俄河以北六英里的地方。一个好心的贵格会教友正悄悄地对乔希说："躺着，别出声。这里很安全。来了个抓捕

---

abolitionist *n.* 废奴主义者　　advertisement *n.* 广告

generous *adj.* 宽厚的；仁慈的　　ingrate *n.* 忘恩负义的人

here. Here comes a slave-catcher, but I know him. I'll talk to him and send him away. You must not fear. None of your brothers and sisters who came to us have ever been taken back to slavery." Then he spoke to the slave-catcher. "Oh, good evening, my friend!" Josh could hear them talking as he ***hid*** in a bag among other bags of corn and potatoes.

It was after ten o'clock that night when Josh's bag was thrown into a wagon and driven away to the next helping hands. And in this way, hiding by day and traveling by night, Josh went north. He was helped all along the way by a few of his own people who had been freed, and always by the good ***Quakers***. And so he made his way to

---

奴隶的，不过，我认识他。我去和他说说话，把他打发走。你千万别怕，你的兄弟姐妹凡是来找我们的，还没有一个被抓回去的。"接着，这位好心人就跟抓捕奴隶的人聊了起来："晚上好，朋友！"乔希能够听到两人说话，他就藏在一个口袋里，混在一堆装着玉米和马铃薯的袋子中。

那天晚上十点过后，乔希藏身的袋子被装进一辆货车里，运到下一个志愿者站点。就这样，乔希昼伏夜出，终于到达了北方。沿途总是能得到仁慈的贵格会教徒的帮助，另有一些帮过他的人是已获自由的黑人同胞。就这样乔希一路来到加拿大。在一个终生难忘的早晨，他终于挺直腰板，

---

hide *v.* 隐藏

Quaker *n.* 教友派信徒

Canada. And on one never—to—be—forgotten morning he stood up straight, ***breathed*** God's air, and knew himself free!

III

To Joshua Leckler, as now he was called, this life in Canada was all new and strange. It was a new thing for him to feel that he was a man like any other man he met among the whites. It was new, too, to be paid what his work was worth. He worked more happily than he had ever done. He was even pleased at how tired his work made him feel.

Sometimes there came to his ears stories of his brothers and sisters in the South. Often he met ***escaped*** slaves like himself. Their

---

呼吸到了自由的空气，知道自己从此获得了自由！

III

对约书亚·莱柯勒（乔希的现名）来说，在加拿大的生活真是新鲜而又奇特。现在，他觉得自己是一个人，和碰到的那些白人没什么两样，这可是以前从未有过的感觉。干多少活就拿多少钱，这也是一种全新的体验。他干起活来比以往任何时候都更加开心，哪怕是累得筋疲力尽，也心甘情愿。

有时，他也听到一些有关南方同胞的情况，也常常碰到像他一样逃出来的奴隶。这些人悲伤的经历激起了他的欲望，使他渴望做些什么以帮助

---

breathe *v.* 呼吸　　**escape** *v.* 逃跑

sad stories made him ***burn*** to do something to help people he had left behind him. But these escaped slaves, and the newspapers he read, told him other things, too. They said that the idea of freedom was rising in the United States. Already, people were speaking out about ***abolishing*** slavery and freeing the slaves. Already people were helping those abolitionist leaders like Sumner, Phillips, Douglass, Garrison. Joshua heard the names Lucretia Mott and Harriet Beecher Stowe. And Joshua was hopeful, for after the long night of slavery he saw the first light of morning.

So the years passed. Then from those dark clouds of slavery the storm of war broke: the thunder of guns and the rain of ***bullets***. From

---

身后那些仍在受苦受难的人们。但是这些逃出来的奴隶，还有他读到的报纸，也给他带来了其他一些信息：在美国，自由的观念已成燎原之势，人们已经在大胆地谈论废除奴隶制、解放奴隶，并开始帮助那些废奴主义领袖，如萨姆纳、菲利普斯、道格拉斯、加里森等。约书亚还听到了卢克利希亚·莫特和哈利特·比彻的名字。约书亚满怀希望，因为经历了奴隶制的漫漫长夜之后，他看到了黎明的第一线曙光。

时光飞逝。在奴隶制的阴云笼罩下，终于刮起了战争的风暴。一时间枪林弹雨，炮声隆隆。约书亚身处北方家中，密切关注着战争的动向。时局时而有利于北方，时而有利于南方。这时，从战争风暴中突然传来一

---

burn *v.* 激起

abolish *v.* 废除

bullet *n.* 子弹

his home in the North Joshua watched the storm. Sometimes the war went well for the North, sometimes for the South. Then suddenly out from the storm came a cry like the voice of God, "You and your brothers and sisters are free!" Free, free, with freedom for all—not just for a few. Freedom for all who had been ***enslaved***. Not free by escaping in the night—free to live in the light of morning.

When the northern army first ***called for*** black ***soldiers***, Joshua went to Boston to sign up. Since he could read and write, and because of his general intelligence, he was soon made an ***officer***. One day Mr. Leckler saw a list of names of these black soldiers. His eyes stopped at the name "Joshua Leckler." He showed the list to Mrs. Leckler.

个如同上帝的声音："你和你的兄弟姐妹们全都自由了！"自由了，自由了，是所有的人，不是少数人，全都自由了。所有被奴役的人全都自由了。人们无须靠暗夜逃亡去获得自由，而是在晨光中尽情地享受自由。

当北军第一次号召黑人参战时，约书亚就去波士顿应征入伍了。由于能读书写字，加之聪明能干，他很快就被擢升为军官。一天，莱柯勒先生看到了一张黑人士兵名单。他的目光停在了"约舒亚·莱柯勒"的名字上。他把这份名单拿给莱柯勒夫人看。

---

enslave *v.* 使某人成为奴隶
call for 号召
soldier *n.* 军人；士兵
officer *n.* 军官

"Mrs. Leckler," he said, "look what happened because I taught a black to read and write. I disobeyed the law of my ***state***. I lost my slave. And I gave the Yankees a smart officer to help them fight the war. I was wrong—I was wrong. But I am right, too, Mrs. Leckler. This all happened because of my ***generous*** heart, and your bad ***advice***. But oh, that ingrate, that ingrate!"

"莱柯勒夫人，"他说："看看吧，就因为我教会了一个黑人读书写字，结果竟是这个样子。我违背了本州的法律，我失去了我的奴隶。我给北佬培养了一个聪明的军官来帮助他们作战。我错了，我真是大错特错了。但我的做法也没有什么不对的，莱柯勒夫人。发生这一切都怪我心太好，还有你那个糟糕的忠告。不过，那小子忘恩负义，真是忘恩负义啊！"

---

state *n.* 州

generous *adj.* 宽宏大量的

advice *n* 忠告；建议